The Color of HOPE
African American Mental Health in the Church

Copyright 2020 by Pamela Robinson, DMin, MDiv, LLMSW, BSW

All rights reserved. No part of this publication may be reproduced or transmitted in any form or by any means, electronic or mechanical, including photocopying, recording or by any information storage and retrieval system, without permission in writing from the publisher.

This book was originally a dissertation completed for
Apex School of Theology entitled:
*Educating the African American Church Toward
Those with Disabilities to Have an Attitudinal Change.*

A project thesis submitted to the faculty of Apex School of Theology in partial fulfillment for the Degree of Doctor of Ministry in Biblical Studies
Durham, North Carolina

In collaboration with Fortitude Graphic Design & Printing and
Season Press, LLC

Scripture quotations taken from the Holy Bible, New International Version NIV Copyright @ 1973, 1978, 1984, 2011 by Biblica, Inc. TM Used by permission. All rights reserved worldwide. www.zondervan.com The "KJV" are trademarks registered in the United States Patent and
Trademark Office by Biblica, Inc.

Neither the author nor the publisher is engaged in rendering medical services, mental health services, or professional advice in this book. The reader is encouraged to consult his or her medical, health, financial, or other competent professional before adopting any of the suggestions in this book or drawing inferences from it. Neither the author nor the publisher shall be liable or responsible for any loss or damage allegedly arising from any information or suggestions in this book. While the author has made every effort to provide accurate telephone and internet addresses at the time of publication, neither the publisher nor the author assumes any responsibility for errors or changes that occur after publication.

The Color of HOPE: African American Mental Health in the Church/
Pamela Robinson, DMin, MDiv, LLMSW, BSW
p. cm
1. Mental Health—United States 2. African American Mental Health—United States 3. African American Church response of— United States
ISBN-13: 978-1-7353600-3-4
First Edition
10 9 8 7 6 5 4 3 2
Printed in United States of America

DEDICATION

To my parents, Willie Clarence and Bessie Mae Haymon, Sr., thank you for teaching me to believe in myself, in God, and in my dreams.

To Emmanuel and Laura Mae Saunders, my maternal grandparents. Your history is remembered in the laughter and tears of your children and their children's children. It is in me that your history becomes a future.

To my loving husband, Curtis, for always encouraging me to go on every adventure, especially this one. You are someone I can trust, be myself with, and can depend on.

To my children Andrea Latrice, Jermaine Maurice, and Carmela Denise Harris for your never-ending support, encouragement, and belief in my dreams. To the memory of my beloved brother Willie Clarence Haymon, Jr. Your guiding light and infinite faith continues to sustain me.

To my precious Zecaryah Bjorn Barker for bringing so much joy into my life. You will always be the one who took my heart by surprise. You will always be my FIRST grandchild; a true blessing from above.

TABLE OF CONTENTS

Acknowledgements	xiii
Foreword	xvii
Introduction	xxi
Chapter One – *Am I Out of Place?*	1
Chapter Two - *Hidden in Plain Sight*	13
Chapter Three - *The Black Church: A Change Agent*	31
Chapter Four - *Facing Unique Challenges*	39
Chapter Five - *Mistrust*	53
Chapter Six - *The HOPE Culturally Centered Model (HCCM)*	59
History	69
Appendices	82
Definitions	104
Reference List	107
Recommended Reading	113
About the Author	114
Book Reviews	116

Acknowledgements

In Loving Memory

Willie C. Haymon, Jr., your special gift of compassion and your loving spirit wove deep into my inner being. Thank you for being my spiritual mentor and for being the best big brother a girl could ever hope for. You were someone that I looked up to for wisdom and Godly advice throughout my entire life. You always pushed education and was willing to share your knowledge and skills with all who came in contact with you.

Even through your terminal illness, you encouraged me to finish my goal of completing my Doctorate degree. Your example kept me working even harder when I wanted to give up. I will forever reflect on your courage, determination, and strength that was reflected by your modest, humble, and loving spirit. Your legacy of high standards, morals and values touched and inspired many in our family and in the community.

Special Thanks

Momma and Daddy, I owe everything to you. You lived in a time that is outside my scope of understanding, confronting, and defeating obstacles with grace and dignity. I know that my existence in the world I grew up in would have been hopeless had I not been blessed to be the daughter of Willie Clarence and Bessie Mae Haymon, Sr. You were the personification of all that is strong, selfless, powerful, compassionate, and determined. In all my accomplishments, significant and insignificant, I thank and love you both with all my heart.

Curtis L. Robinson, Sr., my devoted husband. Thank you for being a part of this entire process. Your warm spirit and unshakable calm during my stormy hours have been the blessing and balance I needed to complete this crucial work. From the beginning, you were there and now, in the end, I salute you for hanging in there with me. Thank you for your genuine, authentic, and unconditional love. From my heart I will always be thankful for your support.

Andrea Harris, my precious first-born young adult child. Your ability to dream without walls is a constant reminder to me that "I can do all things through Christ Jesus that strengthens me." Your resiliency is contagious! Continue to dream big and get big results.

Jermaine Harris, my amazing son. I will always cherish our strong mother and son bond. Do not limit yourself because of other people's limited imaginations. Always be a first-rate version of YOURSELF, instead of a second-rate version of somebody else.

Carmela Harris, my beautiful youngest daughter. Your wisdom far exceeds your age. Thank you for inspiring me to look deeper within myself. Always be kind to yourself, you are your own best friend.

Curtis, Tiffany, and Timothy, my adult stepchildren. Thank you for the sincere love, kindness, and respect you have shown me. I am deeply grateful to be your stepmother.

Marilyn Haymon, my sister-n-law. Your unwavering support, encouragement, long talks on the phone, listening to me as I cried, complained, and expressed a gamut of emotions, will always be cherished. Thank you for your love and support even as your husband, my beloved brother Willie, experienced Multiple Myeloma (Bone Cancer) before his transition. I genuinely appreciate your sisterhood over the past 35 years . . . you are God sent.

With Gratitude

This book was originally a dissertation completed for Apex School of Theology entitled: *Educating the African American Church Toward Those with Disabilities to Have an Attitudinal Change*. The project thesis was submitted to the faculty of Apex School of Theology in partial fulfillment for the Degree of Doctor of Ministry in Biblical Studies, Durham, North Carolina. Consequentially, turning my dissertation into a book was one of the hardest things I have ever done in my career. It was a long, arduous, and often solitary process, requiring hours of work and multiple drafts. Unquestionably, I have enjoyed the challenging process of writing my first book.

I am grateful to Dr. Lafayette Maxwell and the entire staff at the Apex School of Theology for the opportunity to become a student in the doctorate program. I thank the faculty for their encouragement and guidance, which gave birth to the idea for my project document. I give credit to the Late Dr. Joseph E. Perkins, founder of Apex School of Theology, and his wife, Dr. Carrie Perkins, Dr. Lafayette Maxwell, Dr. Cornelius Battle, and Dr. Gladys Long. Thanks are also due to Ms. Rolanda Holland, Mr. Joseph Perkins, Jr. Mr. Anthony Patterson, Mrs. Floya Brown, Mrs., Juretta Ruffin, Ms. Sandra Manning, Dr. Harry Lawson, Dr. Clarence Burke, Dr. Henry Wells, Ms. Gloria Dunston, Mrs. Joyce Hayward, Mrs. Brenda Harris for their help and support.

I would also like to thank my Professional Associates: the Elder Dr. Reginald High, Dr. Jerry Grimes, Dr. Herbert Davis, Dr. George Daniels, Dr. M. Andrew Davis, Dr. Allred Marshall, Dr. Mary Morgan, and Dr. Carol Bunch and Dr. Sharon Lee for all their brilliant editing, comments, and suggestions for improvement. To my former Pastor Reverend Dr. Michael T. Scott, Sr., (Pastor of Galilee Baptist Church Kalamazoo, Michigan), for his support and participation in the doctoral research project, I offer my sincerest appreciation.

I give thanks to those who gave me their abiding support and assistance on this journey to completion. To my doctoral committee members and professional associates: Dr. Lafyette Maxwell, Dr. Gladys Long, Dr. Cornelius Battle, Dr. Luchara Wallace, Dr. Michael T. Scott, Sr., Dr. Tamara Scott, Contextual Associates: Pastor Curtis L. Robinson, Mr. Jermaine Harris, Elder Dorla Bonner-Colemen, and Minister Barrett Lee, and to my Peer Associate Dr. Janet Harris for a job well done in your support, time, and dedication to my research. Words are not enough to express my appreciation for all that you have done and continue to do in support of my efforts.

Most of all, I thank the Lord for the strength, wisdom, and knowledge to put this research on paper and convert my solid dissertation into a publishable book. May my sacrifices bring glory to the Kingdom.

To God be the Glory,

Pamela Robinson, DMin, MDiv, LLMSW, BSW

Foreword
Dr. Lafayette Maxwell

The Color of HOPE is a must-read not just for the African American Church community but for all people, denominations, and ethnicities. Those who are caregivers and care receivers from all walks of life, whether in family, communities, or schools, can benefit from this book, which will help us broaden our own understanding of how to help those who are dealing with these maladies. Moreover, this book will serve as a guide to develop and assist us in our churches, community ministries, and organizations. Dr. Pamela and Rev. Curtis L. Robinson's goal is to normalize and not marginalize those with mental health issues.

Dr. Pamela Robinson's book will challenge us to deal with the "elephant in the room," concerning those who struggle with mental health issues. The Church can become stakeholders by socially networking with nonprofit organizations that are committed to educating, and equipping, and empowering the churches and agencies to encourage and better the lives of the caregivers and the care receivers. This couple is using the Therapeutics approach which is a "person-centered solution focused, practical, reality-oriented, and collaborative perspective that focuses on solutions, and not problems."

This book was birthed and enhanced at Apex School of Theology in Durham, North Carolina, where I served as The Dean of the Doctoral Studies Program and Chief Academic Officer. Dr. Pamela and Rev. Robinson joined us in August 2015 through May 2017 and the two graduated with honors. They worked together on her dissertation, *Educating the African American Church Toward Those with Disabilities to Have an Attitudinal Change*. Dr. Robinson's dissertation examined the attitude of an Urban African American Congregation toward adults ages 18-25 with mental challenges, to benefit the church and community by increasing the membership and discipleship through involvement in ministry, and to enhance and equip the church to fulfill its mission of the kerygma found in Matthew 28;19-20.

In May of 2017, Dr. Robinson was conferred a Doctor of Ministry Degree in Biblical Studies during the Apex School of Theology Commencement Ceremony in Durham, NC. After graduation, both Dr. Pamela and Rev. Robinson came back to Apex School of Theology as our special guest to present her dissertation with Apex School of Theology and the Durham Community.

Finally, I would encourage all those who are caregivers to purchase this book as a guide to help churches develop a Christian-based ministry in their church body. When, together, faith-based communities, mental health agencies, stakeholders, service providers, community members, and individual families address the issues brought forth in *The Color of HOPE,* it will:

- Increase our awareness of mental health challenges and its impact on the lives of the caregiver and the care receiver.
- Identify mental health resources and services in the community and offer powerful and creative ministries of spiritual support, and
- Use culturally-crowned committees consisting of clergy, mental health professionals, laypeople, individuals and their families, and churches.

Dr. Lafayette Maxwell is former Dean of the Doctor of Ministry Program and Chief Academic Officer of Apex School of Theology, Durham, North Carolina.

Foreword
Luchara Wallace, Ph.D.

It is such an honor to be able to write a few words of acknowledgement on the behalf of Dr. Pamela Robinson as she presents her first book, *The Color Of HOPE: African American Mental Health in the Church*. Dr. Robinson's vision for this book evolved from her dissertation project, *Educating the African American Church Toward those with Disabilities to have an Attitudinal Change*, which measured the familiarity of members of an African American church congregation with the nature and presence of disability and mental health needs within the faith community. It was truly an honor to serve on Dr. Robinson's dissertation committee and as her local chair as she developed and executed her research.

In a masterful fashion, Dr. Robinson engaged in survey research, group interviews, and appealed to the spirit of the congregation through a sermonic soliloquy. She educated, challenged, and elevated how the congregation viewed and understood members with disability and/or who might experience mental health challenges.

According to Dr. Robinson, *The Color of HOPE* will help you to better understand individuals in your faith community who experience mental health challenges, normalize the situation for that person, and broaden your own understanding of mental health disorders especially among the Christian community. This book is revolutionary because it seeks to address the many challenges faith communities experience when attempting to meaningfully integrate members with mental health disorders into the congregation.

Frequently, issues surrounding mental health are treated as taboo topics. *The Color of HOPE* addresses those issues head on and provides concrete steps on how to be a more responsive ministry, and most importantly, with HOPE. *The Color of HOPE* was written for physicians, psychiatrists, psychologists, therapists, mental health professionals, individuals with mental illness and their loved ones, and those who are interested in the topic.

Although this book evolved out of Dr. Robinson's dissertation, its roots lie in her life and ministry. As a Licensed Clinical Social Worker, Dr. Robinson is the co-pastor and founder of Emerging HOPE Ministries and Emerging HOPE Christian Counseling, which provides culturally-relevant pastoral care, mental health services and programming in partnership with clients.

The Color of HOPE gives hope, guidance, and concrete methods to incorporate into ministries committed to the inclusion of individuals with mental health disorders.

>Luchara Wallace, Ph.D.
>Director, Lewis Walker Institute for the Study of Race and Ethnic Relations, Western Michigan University; Principal Investigator and Director, School Connection Program; and Associate Professor, Special Education, WMU College of Education & Human Development

Introduction

"We realized that the truth we had discovered was not being served by the way in which we were describing it. We needed a language that told the truth, in the way that it had been told to us by black people everywhere."

The late Dr. Price M. Cobbs, an internationally-recognized psychiatrist, author, and management consultant best known as coauthor of Black Rage, regarded by the New York Times as "one of the most important books on blacks."

How great is the love the father has lavished on us, that we should be called children of God.
1 John 3:1 King James Version

According to the Pew Forum on Religion and Public Life, a demographic study of the religious landscape in the United States reported that African Americans have the greatest degree of religious belief among all the racial-ethic groups (Pew Research Center 2015). Specifically, 97% of all African Americans reported belief in God, with 83% reporting belief in God with absolute certainty, and 75% of African Americans reported religion was very important in their lives, compared with 53% of people in the general population. While African American families may assist family members faced with psychiatric problems, this data suggests that Black churches are valuable places to implement mental health interventions for their population.

Despite high rates of religious attendance and importance, African Americans fail to fully utilize professional mental health services relative to their White counterparts (Hankerson et al. 2011). Factors that contribute to these racial treatment disparities include distrust of providers, limited access to care, financial constraints, high attrition rates, and stigma of mental illness (Hankerson et al., 2015). African Americans who do seek professional treatment are more likely to receive lower-quality care and significantly less likely to receive guideline-concordant care (Gonzalez et al., 2010). Given the enormous individual and societal cost associated with mental disorders (Murray and Lopez 1997), exploring the role of African American faith-based organizations is an essential component of Black mental health.

There is an ongoing need for advocacy for individuals with mental health challenges who attend African American churches, as well as a need to continue to raise awareness about the social stigma these individuals encounter. Stigma has complex roots in society and often goes unnoticed and unaddressed. Stigma complicates the process of recovery for patients for many reasons and it also interferes with their willingness to seek professional help due to a fear of being labeled, misunderstood, or judged as having a lack of faith.

Those who have a family member with mental illness may not know where to turn for help. Understanding and coping with the illness, as well as the search for services and support, may drain them spiritually, physically, emotionally, and financially. Often, relationships with extended family members and friends are strained. The illness itself and the associated stigma of mental illness can lead to feelings of guilt, denial, grief, isolation, and loss of hope.

People who live with mental illness are disproportionately impacted by the social injustices. These injustices may include prejudice, poverty, inadequate housing, unemployment or underemployment. In addition they may face lack of access to health care (especially mental health care) and inequalities within the criminal justice system.

> *Incline your ear, and come unto me: hear, and your soul shall live; and I will make an everlasting covenant with you, even the sure mercies of David.*
> **Isaiah 55:3**

Of all the characters of the Old Testament, King David is the most closely related to Jesus Christ – not only as a forefather but as a 'shadow' or 'type' of Jesus to come. "Son of David" was the first title given to Jesus (Matt.1:1), and in one of his last statements, Jesus said,"I am the Root and Offspring of David" (Rev. 22:16). Acts 13:22 states that God "found David . . . a man after my own heart."

David certainly had amazing abilities such as courage, strength, musical ability, and great leadership skills. But the quality of David's character that most fully represents Jesus is found in the story recorded in 2 Samuel 9:1-13, the story of Mephibosheth, son of Jonathan, grandson of Saul. David's motivation in his actions toward Mephibosheth had nothing to do with elevating himself in the eyes of others. It was all about kindness, compassion, mercy –

three of the translations of the Hebrew word khehsed, also translated "steadfast love" and "loving kindness" to represent God's love.

David initiated the relationship with Mephibosheth and did everything for him. In the same way, God initiates the relationship with each of us; Jesus said: "No one can come to me unless the Father who sent me draws them" (John 6:44). David takes no notice of Mephibosheth's disablement. He took him as he was. Back then, lameness was a social disgrace, a sin. Yet David regarded it not. All of us have entered this world crippled with sin. We can do nothing to remove this sin in our own strength. We are all Mephibosheths who experience the compassion of Jesus. He calls each of us by name.

Moreover, each of us has entered this world with some type of ailment. There are times in each of our lives when we may need a shoulder to lean on. Therefore, with this in passage of scripture as the premise for my passion, I conducted a study to examine the beliefs and behaviors of an African American faith community toward adults with mental illness. I, in turn, created a service model that is the theoretical underpinning for this book.

The study comprised a series of (mental health focused) sermonic presentations, a congregational survey, focus groups, educational workshops, webinars, and community outreach events. The research was a pilot of a multi-model approach to incorporating members with mental illness into an inclusive context. This would be achieved by educating parishioners about mental illness and disabilities while presenting the content from a faith-based perspective.

The primary objective involved assessments, perceptions, attitudes, education, prevention, group support, and treatment for using the Statistical Manual of Mental Disorders (DSM–5)or its correlates. The number of participants were reported, qualitative data was reported, and African Americans were the target population. Although the study was limited by a small sample size, there is an emerging opportunity for predominantly African American churches to provide concrete mental health services.

Clergy have an invaluable role in the U.S. mental healthcare delivery system. Findings from the National Comorbidity Survey, a nationally representative general population survey of 8,098 adults in the United States, showed that a higher percentage of people sought help for mental disorders from clergy (25%) compared with psychiatrists (16.7%) or general medical doctors (16.7%) (Want et al., 2003). Clergy provide the only source of mental health care for many low-income patients (Molock et al., 2008).

> "At the root of this dilemma is the way we view mental health in this country. Whether an illness effects your heart, your leg or your brain, it's still an illness, and there should be no distinction."
>
> *Michelle Obama*

African American clergy in particular are the primary source of mental healthcare for socioeconomically diverse adults and are trusted "gatekeepers" for referrals to mental health specialists. In one study, approximately 50% of African Americans utilizing only one source of mental healthcare sought help from clergy providers. A detailed analysis of African American clergy in a large city revealed that clergy averaged more than six hours of counseling work per week and often addressed serious problems similar to those seen by secular mental health professionals (Young et al., 2003).

African American churches can be tremendous help, offering hope, unconditional love, and support to people who often find themselves stigmatized and isolated from the community. Persons with a mental illness and their families frequently turn first to clergy for answers to this severe crisis in their lives. The illness can raise profound questions concerning God and faith. The African American church response can make a difference in people's reactions to the crisis and their recovery from it.

Since society in general has shirked its responsibility for adequate care of those who face serious mental illness, it is critical for African American churches to speak for those who often have no voice in the community The church also should seek compassion for those affected and justice for what is rightfully theirs. The African American church is called upon not only to reach out to individuals and their families but also to bring about change in the systemic problems facing the mental health delivery system (Lambert, 2015).

Churches are like a stained-glass window. When we see a stained-glass window in a church, we are struck by the beauty of the story it tells. The window usually depicts a story from scripture or an aspect of our faith. Taken as a whole, the window gives a complete picture of a story or inspiring moment. When we approach the window and look closely at the art, we see that the window is made up of many pieces of glass. The pieces have different shapes and sizes, some are large, and some are tiny. We see that the pieces are made of different colors.

Upon closer inspection, we see that the pieces have flaws in them, some have lines or cracks, others have tiny air bubbles in the glass. But taken together as a whole, the unique pieces, big and small of various colors, with all their flaws, transcend their individuality and come together at the hand of the artist. This in turn gives a dynamic story of faith. But what happens if part of the window is missing? What if we were to remove all the brown pieces of glass, or remove the large pieces, or the ones with bubbles in them?

The picture would not get the whole story. The body of Christ and the faith community, in one sense, is like a stained-glass window. It lives the story of redemption and salvation in the reality of everyday life. The pieces of the story are made up of many kinds and sorts of people, young elderly people, married people and single people, people of color, people of different shapes and sizes, people who are divorced, people with mental illness, and people with various disabilities. Like the stained-glass window, the body of Christ is made up of many parts. If we intentionally or unintentionally exclude, discriminate against, or ignore one or more parts, we do not get the whole picture; we are missing the full, complete story.

For people with mental illness the societal stigma and misperceptions of the disease often keep people from participating in church. Some may feel the stigma and misperception by society has entered into the hearts and minds of those in their own community of faith. Church, rather than mirroring the cultural biases of society should challenge those assumptions and in turn accept and reach out to all people, to open doors and minds to the gifts of all God's people. Churches that truly welcome and include everyone in a proactive way portray the story of redemption and salvation as a clear and beautiful image of God's Kingdom (Lambert, 2017).

Since mental illness is hidden and not readily apparent, it takes on an even greater urgency for ministry. Persons with mental illness are vulnerable and discriminated against in the workplace, in housing opportunities, and in the healthcare system. If ever there was a mission for the African American church, outreach to persons with mental illness and their families is one!

> *Have I not commanded you? Be strong and courageous. Do not be frightened, and do not be dismayed, for the Lord your God is with you wherever you go.*
> **Joshua 1:9**

The Color of HOPE
African American Mental Health in the Church

"The flower that blooms in adversity is the greatest of them all."
Mulan the Motion Picture

Pamela Robinson
DMin, MDiv, LLMSW, BSW

We Wear the Mask
*We wear the mask that grins and lies,
It hides our cheeks and shades our eyes,—
This debt we pay to human gulle;
With torn and bleeding hearts we smile,
And mouth with myrlad subtleties.
Why should the world be over-wise,
In counting all our tears and sighs?
Nay, let them only see us, while
We wear the mask.
We smile, but, O great Christ, our cries
To thee from tortured souls arise.
We sing, but oh the clay is vile
Beneath our feet, and long the mile;
But let the world think other-wise,
We wear the mask!*

*Poet Maya Angelou adapted Paul Dunbar's
"We Wear the Mask"*

Chapter 1
Am I Out of Place?

Where do you belong? Who do you belong to?

The answer to those questions may not be as straightforward to many as they will be for Christians. A sense of belonging is something that many people crave, especially in a world where the feeling of disconnection from others is commonplace, and displacement is a huge problem. Modern technology, mobility, the current refugee crisis, and the COVID-19 Pandemic have millions of people asking similar questions.

For those who feel isolated because of their lack of meaningful relationships and those who feel out of place in foreign surroundings, the solutions to their problems seem rooted in meeting a criterion. The possession of a desired set of characteristics could help someone who is feeling lonely be welcomed into a social group. And acquiring the necessary social graces can help the displaced move to a place which they feel they belong.

In both instances, the connection is temporary. To establish a permanent sense of belonging, we must look beyond people and places. What we discover through Jesus is that belonging is about so much more than a relationship with some*thing*, it is about a relationship with some*one*. And what is so inspiring about belonging to Jesus is that we do not need to fit a certain criterion. He welcomes us no matter who we are, where we are from and what we have done.

There were times in my childhood that I felt lonely, isolated, misunderstood, and out of place. I tried desperately to minimize the things that made me feel different. I would sit on our front porch and imagine that I never experienced deep loss. It was an emotional emptiness that I could not articulate due to my emotional development.

At the age of 3, when I just started to understand who I was, what I was feeling, and what to expect when interacting with others, my mother died. For years she suffered from chronic asthma. Sadly, at the tender age of 36, she died as a result of the disease. I was the second youngest of seven children she left alone in the world. We were ages 2 through 14 and were left with a father who soon remarried. My stepmother was a wonderful woman who immediately loved and embraced all seven of us, including my brother who had long-standing undiagnosed mental health challenges. Our Godly stepmother showed each of us unconditional love. She became the mother we all loved dearly. To us, she always will be Mama. She had no biological children of her own until I was 11. Then our youngest brother Gerald was born. Her bond with all her children and my father led to more than 54 years of marriage.

When I was 14, my father accepted "the call" to the ministry. We officially became preacher's kids (a.k.a. PKs). Preaching the gospel was in my father's DNA. He and his nine siblings also were PKs. Their father was a stern Baptist preacher who faithfully served as a pastor for 50 years in rural and urban areas in the deep south. Likewise, several of my father's brothers were pastors and most of his siblings were devote Christians.

My father was the sole provider in our home. Although he never completed a high school education, he was a proponent of education. He attended night school to learn a trade as a Lathe Operator to increase his income so that he could better care for our family. As a blue-collar factory worker, he took great pride in his job. He worked for one employer for forty-one years. I cannot assume that it was an all smooth ride, however, he stayed the course. Through his strong work ethic and Christian values, he was a Godly man who showed unconditional love for our family, church family, friends, and community members. Oftentimes, he showed love to those whom some may have felt didn't deserve it. I liken my father's unconditional positive regard to that of the unconditional love of Jesus.

Remember that Jesus was talking to the so-called "bad people" during his days on earth, yet he was aware of the listening ears of the so-called "good people." Remember that the prodigal was descriptive of the "bad people" with whom Jesus was associating. Like a loving father, Jesus welcomed them into his arms and was more concerned with their futures than with their pasts.

Today, it seems, we have an incredible amount of expectation of one another. The idea of unconditional love seems to have fallen by the wayside as more and more of us want love, but are ill-prepared to give or even receive it. To love someone under any circumstance is a true test of unconditional loving. Although it may seem simple, it is probably one of the toughest attributes to possess. This kind of love requires an unconditional love of yourself first, so you can have the strength of heart and mind to give the same to another human being. This is where we fall down.

Within our society, there seems to be so much pressure to be perfect that to love ourselves has become a pretty hard task to achieve. But, it is the key to total, unconditional love of all others. The Bible story of the Prodigal Son is an example. The parable in Luke 11:15-32 ends with a son who returned home after squandering his inheritance. However, his father receives him with open arms.

"Father, I have sinned against heaven and against you; I no longer deserve to be called your son." But his father ordered his servants to put the finest robe on his shoulders, a ring on his finger, and sandals on his feet. "Take the fatted calf and slaughter it, and let's have a feast, because this son of mine was dead and has come back to life." Then the celebration began.

Gospel songwriter, Fred Hammond, expresses the unconditional love of a father in his song, "Prodigal Son." Some of the lyrics are as follows:

> *Too many of my days Lord, I've tried to spend there*
> *Searching for what I know was only found in You*
> *I strayed so far away, I wasn't sure You were still there*
> *But deep in my heart was a faint security*
> *And I could almost feel Your open arms*
> *And hear You say to me*
> *Prodigal son, come back to my love*
> *You are the one, that my heart seeks for*
> *Whatever you've done, I cannot even remember*
> *Although there are many in my house*
> *It's still empty without my prodigal son*
> *Have You so much mercy You would pardon me*
> *It's so hard to believe Your love would hide my sins*
> *And even though You take the past far away from me*
> *Could this be a chance to have my place in You again*
> *Speak clear to me Lord that my faith would fully mend*

Will your child be able to return home when he comes to his senses? Will your love for your child overcome your disappointment, your need to judge and your desire to control him or her? Or will you hold on to your pain or hold their mistakes over them? The parable of the prodigal son is clear: God, the Father, does not hold it against us. What then, does this say for us as parents? "When he came to his senses, he said, 'How many of my father's hired servants have food to spare, and here I am starving to death!'" (Luke

15:17).

As Jesus told the story of the lost son, the people hearing it for the first time understood that the younger son's behavior was rebellious and disrespectful. He asked for his inheritance before his father's death. As the son of the landowner, he was also choosing to abandon his community. They understood that this brought shame and embarrassment on the family. Yet, the son did it anyway. The amazing thing about this story is not what the son did, but how the Father responded when the son "came to his senses" and returned home. He embraced him. How did the son know his father would at least take him back at all?

He knew because he knew that his father loved him unconditionally. In his heart, he knew his home was a place of safety, love and security, and that his father would love him no matter what he had done. Remember, always deal with your children the way your heavenly father deals with you. Never break relationship with your child. Always leave the door open and the path to your heart open so your child can return home after he or she sows their wild oats.

My brother Bruce was the third oldest of my eight siblings. If there ever was an example of a Prodigal Son he would fit it perfectly. He was curious, rambunctious, and seemed to be full of mischief. When I was 11, our family observed his issues with sleeplessness, emotional dysregulation, relationships, rebellion, and impaired cognitive abilities. Whether it was his raging, violence, self-harm, or chronic delinquency, my parents knew something was wrong with him.

Moreover, Bruce had a difficult time in the educational system. He would skip school, get into numerous fights, act out in school, and engage in delinquent behavior. On numerous occasions, I recall my parents talking about how the principal called to tell them that Bruce had missed days of school, unbeknownst to them. Bruce felt that no one understood him. He just did not fit in. I can imagine that he may have felt like a social outcast. Unsubstantiated, unquestioned, and inaccurate thoughts and beliefs about him as a Black male student by some of his teachers were harmful and quite detrimental to his negative self image.

The old-age proverb that "sticks and stones may break my bones but words can never hurt me," does not ring true for the effect that believing hurtful words and negative cultural images can have on an individual's mental health. This idea of believing the words is addressed in the concept of internalized racism. Internalized racism refers to the acceptance, by marginalized racial populations, of the negative societal beliefs and stereotypes about themselves. Studies suggest that the internalization of cultural stereotypes by black males can create expectations, anxieties, and reactions that can adversely affect social and psychological functioning.

On several occasions, teachers and counselors suggested that my parents seek mental health treatment for him. Though my parents' intentions were good, they were not aware of the importance of seeking mental health treatment, nor were they willing to entertain the thought of going outside of the church for psychological help. My parents had a different philosophy when it came to addressing mental health issues. It consisted of prayer, church attendance, providing basic needs, and discipline. Therefore, Bruce never saw a psychiatrist, therapist, obtained a diagnosis, or received mental health treatment.

Bruce had been jailed as a result of his mental illness more often than he had been hospitalized to receive treatment. His story illustrates the level of failure in our mental health system but also highlights why some minorities are over-represented in all stages of the criminal justice system.

According to data reviewed by Benjamin Le' Cook Ph.D., senior scientist at the Center for Multicultural Mental Health research at Cambridge Health Alliance, one reason for this is the disparity that exists in the use of mental health services, even though African Americans and Hispanics living in poverty are almost three times more likely to suffer from psychological distress. In fact, African American and Hispanic youth receive 60-50% less attention to their mental health care. Even more tragic than the lack of access to mental health care is what happens as a result.

Due to a lack of mental health treatment, Bruce was in and out of the penitentiary system as a teenager and unfortunately, died in prison at the age of 28. The reported cause of death was suicide, yet, my family was in denial and believed it was foul play on behalf of the prison's personnel. However, a lengthy investigating resulted in unsubstantiated evidence that was presented to our attorney that could not prove whether Bruce was mentally abused or physically neglected. Note that a finding of unsubstantiated does not always mean that maltreatment did not occur. Instead, it may mean that there is not enough evidence to support a finding of substance. Therefore, to this day, our family is uncertain about what really happened to Bruce.

Unfortunately, I can't begin to describe the overwhelming shock, disbelief, anger, helplessness, and disappointment we felt as a family because of my brother's tragic death. I just kept hoping that I would wake up and all of this would be a bad dream. It seems that all my parents thought they had instilled in Bruce from childhood had gone out the window. My parents thought they had their bases covered. Bruce knew God's plan, the blessing of abstaining from sin, and the consequences for carefree living. Where did they go wrong?

My parents said, "I thought God promised us that our son wouldn't rebel. What about Proverbs 22:6, which says, 'Train up a child in the way he should go, even when he is old he will not depart from it'?" They thought, "We trained Bruce up in godly ways, didn't God guarantee that he would not depart from those ways and rebel?"

We must remember that by definition a proverb is a succinct general truth or rule of conduct. It is not a promise. It is important to realize that there is no biblical basis for the assumption that a child's rebelliousness must be the parent's fault. Parents must praise God for His mercy and grace if their children follow the Lord for all of their lives; they must take care not to become puffed up. They must never judge Christian parents whose children do not follow the Lord. None of us want to fall into the sin committed by Job's "comforters."

Because Job was suffering so much, they accused him of having some hidden sin in his life. Parents feel agonizing grief when one of their children becomes rebellious. They feel shame (Proverbs 29:15). It is difficult to know that a child rebelled after so much attention and care has been given to him. Parents feel great disappointment when they feel as if all their efforts, prayers, and their very life seem to have been wasted.

More importantly, my parents questioned themselves, whether they had set a true godly example for Bruce. Undoubtedly, their faith was strong. My father was a charismatic associate minister. Our family practically lived at the church; attending three services every Sunday, and three services throughout the week. Why did God allow this bad thing to happen? How can a God who loved them allow them to experience such great pain and suffering? It just didn't seem to add up. Why didn't they recognize Bruce's fragile mental state as a child and get him the help he needed?

Nevertheless, scripture teaches us that "all things work together for good to them that love God, to them who are the called according to his purpose (Romans 8:28). Consequently, their foremost concern was how would they look in the eyes of others (fear of man), and how could they help their children understand what had taken place? After they asked God for forgiveness, they needed to forgive themselves. The pastor encouraged my parents to avoid bitterness by thanking God for this trail and asking for His wisdom (James 1:2-8). Yet, he never referred them to outside counseling with a licensed culturally-relevant therapist.

God is the author of life. Bruce was in God's mind before the world. God would sovereignly use this situation for good (Roman 8:28), and they had to cling to this truth along with God's other promises. Conversely, God would use this tragedy to draw each member of the family closer to Himself. He knew their heartache and He would comfort and sustain them. He would give them the strength to go through the whole ordeal one day at a time (2 Corinthians 12:9).

Jesus showed us the right way to respond to suffering. In your hard circumstance or tragedy or heartbreaking disappointment, you can learn to respond as Jesus did. As you study God's Word, be alert to Christ's responses when He suffered. Follow His example as God guides you by His Holy Spirit, in each situation you encounter. Through your suffering, you can understand more about your Savior. My brother's life of long unrecognized and untreated mental illness is a painful account of how difficult it is for many people, especially Black men, to speak up and seek help for their own issues. Bruce's life was a lucid and powerful testament to the lifesaving importance of seeking mental health treatment. Sadly, his story is reflective of many in the Black community. There may be millions of men suffering on the inside, but are too afraid to reach out for help.

Mental illness is terrible in its own right, painful, destructive, isolating, often lethal, and frequently tied to alcohol and drug abuse, the suffering and inequity are compounded when experienced by Black men. In the African American community, there is a negative stigma surrounding mental health. Instead of seeking professional help for conditions such as depression and anxiety, many in the community resort to self-medication (drugs, opioids, alcohol, etc.), or isolation in an attempt to solve their problems on their own. This issue of masking pain is especially prevalent amongst Black men.

They grow up in culture that tells them "men are not supposed to cry," or that they "should deal with problems on their own." This only enforces the idea that it's not okay for them to say they are hurting inside. Chimamanda Ngozi Adichie says, "By far, the worst thing we do to males, by making them feel they have to be hard, is that we leave them with very fragile egos. The harder a man feels compelled to be, the weaker his ego is."

Unfortunately, there are countless Black men, out of fear of being labeled as weak or less than a man, who don't want to acknowledge or vocalize any of their pains. In 2020, more than 6.8 million African Americans were diagnosed as having some sort of mental illness. If we are unable to remove the negative stigma surrounding mental health in the community, we are willingly allowing another generation to grow up without access to counseling and mental health improvement resources that can help them live a happy, healthy life.

It has long been established that African Americans demonstrate similar levels of mental illnesses as the majority population, but are much less likely to seek professional mental health services. They also are more likely to terminate treatment early if they do go to a counselor (Corbie-Smith et al., Diala et al., 2000; Snowden, 1999; Thompson et al., 2004). A host of factors have been implicated in this disparity. They include stigma about mental health, past negative experiences, strong family units, sense of pride, and lack of economic resources, to name a few.

One interesting finding is that African Americans tend to go to religious leaders for counseling rather than psychological professionals. This is not surprising considering the high proportion of African Americans who assert religious affiliations (Frazier et al., 2005; McMinn et al., 1998; Weaver et al., 2003). However, quantitative studies that measured the seeking of psychological or other mental health services on a large scale give us little qualitative information about the nature and quality of those services. Qualitative studies that give more detailed information are generally on a smaller scale and therefore are not very generalizable to the larger population.

Mental Health Care, Not Jail

"We know a heck of a lot more about why and how and where black men fail than we do about how and why they are successful."
James Minor, Southern Education Foundation

Current research supports that African Americans are overrepresented on almost every criminal justice statistic. Several studies indicate that there are racial biases in the punishment for at least some crimes. Before the Civil War, laws in the United States explicitly provided more severe punishments for Blacks that for Whites who were guilty of the same crime. Such legal statutes no longer exist, yet the administration of justice is still especially harsh to Blacks when the victim is White. There is overwhelming evidence that the criminal justice system is racist.

Majorities of both races in America say Black people are treated less fairly than Whites in dealings with the police, and by the criminal justice system as a whole. In a 2019 Center survey, 84% of Black adults said that, in dealing with police, they are generally treated less fairly than Whites; 63% of Whites agree. Similarly, 87% of Blacks and 61% of Whites said the U.S. criminal justice system treats African Americans less fairly. Negative stereotypes of African Americans as violent criminals has led to the widespread use of race in the creation of law enforcement profiles. According, to be Black—especially to be a young Black male, makes one a suspect.

Psychological Cost

Literature suggests high level of police surveillance may be an important but neglected source of stress in the lives of many African Americans. The threat of a humiliating encounter with law enforcement officers may lead to high levels of psychological arousal. Qualitative research and journalistic accounts suggest that many African Americans engage in a broad range of anticipatory coping strategies to avoid or minimize exposure to discriminatory experiences, including encounters with the police. The psychological cost, if any, of this heightened vigilance have not been systematically addressed.

Clearly there is a need to trace and assess the mental health consequences of the Black population's high level of involvement with the criminal justice system. The high rates of exposure violent crimes, homicide, police harassment, and incarceration are all fraught with mental health consequences that are not yet well understood. Problems such as suicidal ideation and attempts, psychosomatic symptoms, depression, drug, and alcohol abuse have all been reported to stem from a racially biased criminal justice system.

Serious mental illness has become so prevalent in the U.S. Corrections System that jails and prisons are now commonly called "the new asylums." In point of fact, the jails in Los Angeles County, Chicago's Cook County, or New York's Riker's Island, each hold more mentally ill inmates than any remaining psychiatric hospital in the United States. Overall, approximately 20% of inmates in jails and 15% of inmates in state prisons are now estimated to have a serious mental illness.

Based on the total inmate population, this means approximately 383,000 individuals with severe psychiatric disease were behind bars in the United States in 2014, or nearly ten times the number of patients remaining in the nation's state hospitals. In Florida's Orange County jail, the average stay for all inmates is 26 days; for mentally ill inmates, it is 51 days. In New York's Riker's Island, the average stay for all inmates is 42 days; for mentally ill inmates, it is 215 days.

The main reason mentally ill inmates are incarcerated longer than other prisoners is that many find it difficult to understand and follow jail and prison rules. In one study, jail inmates were twice as likely (19% versus 9%) to be charged with facility rule violations. In another study, in Washington state prisons, mentally ill inmates accounted for 41% of infractions even though they constituted only 19% of the prison population (Eliminating Barriers to the Treatment of Mental Illness, 2016).

Additionally, pretrial inmates with serious mental illness experience longer incarcerations than other inmates in many states if they require an evaluation or restoration of competency to stand trial. A survey of state hospital officials in 2015 found that 78% of the 40 responding states were wait-listing pretrial inmates for hospital services. The waits were "in the 30-day range" in most states, but three states reported forensic bed waits of six months to one year. Mentally ill inmates in some states are reported to spend more time waiting for competency restoration so they can be tried than they would spend behind bars convicted of the offense for which they have been charged (Eliminating Barriers to the Treatment of Mental Illness, 2016).

While in prison, mentally-ill inmates are more likely to commit suicide. It is the leading cause of death in correctional facilities, and multiple studies indicate as many as half of all inmate suicides are committed by the estimated 15 % to 20% of inmates with serious mental illness. A 2002 study in the state of Washington found that the prevalence of mental illness among inmates who attempted suicide was 77%, compared with 15% [among inmates] in the general jail population (Serious Mental Illness Prevalence in Jails and Prisons, 2016). The *Los Angeles Times* headlined: "Jail Suicides Reach Record Pace in State," and added: "Some experts blame the recent surge on forcing more of the mentally ill behind bars," (Johnson, 2002).

With the rising rates of incarceration in the United States much needs to be done to address the psychological wellbeing of offenders. Our community mental health system, crisis system and laws are antiquated, fragmented and do not reflect modern research and science. What other illness is it okay to discharge people in the middle of the night, homeless, psychotic, and then arrest them when we don't provide them with the services they need? This is a shameful American tragedy and it is one that must be reversed examined the relationship between the overall rate of psychiatric disorders and suicides in the nation's largest state prison population.

Texas Department of Criminal Justice inmates who were incarcerated for any duration between September 2006 and September 2007 were analyzed by Poisson regression, to assess the independent associations of major psychiatric disorders and demographic characteristics with suicide. Across the entire study cohort, 41 inmates (18 per 100,000) were reported to have committed suicide during the 12-month follow-up period; 21 of them had a diagnosis of a serious mental illness. An elevated risk of suicide was observed among inmates with major depressive disorder (relative risk [RR] = 5.1, 95% confidence interval [CI] = 1.9-13.8), bipolar disorder (RR = 4.6, CI = 1.3-15.9), and schizophrenia (RR = 7.3, CI = 1.7-15.9).

The highest overall risk was present in those inmates with a nonschizophrenic psychotic disorder (RR = 13.8, CI = 5.8-32.9). These findings highlight the importance of maintaining suicide prevention programs in correctional settings, with particular emphasis on screening and monitoring of patients with severe psychiatric disorders (Baillargeon et al., 2009).

Blessed be the God and Father of our Lord Jesus Christ, the Father of mercies and God of all comfort; who comforts us in all our affliction so that we may be able to comfort those who are in any affliction with comfort with which we ourselves are comforted by God.
2 Corinthians 1:3-4

Over the years, I'd learned that under the bed was the best place to keep anything I didn't want found, because there was so much crap— papers, magazines, dirty socks, grocery bags— that no one would ever suspect that anything of value was under there. Sort of like hiding in plain sight.
Kristin Walker, author

Chapter 2
Hidden in Plain Sight

Ezra showed up at an outdoor concert toward the beginning of today following a chaotic plane trip. Having spent his last few dollars to purchase a sandwich, he was broke and hungry. As Ezra proceeded toward the massive crowds that were gathering at the concert; he seemed to be in some type of fog. He heard things that were not there and believed that something was controlling his thoughts.

He could not seem to get his thoughts together. His head felt as if it was spinning. The voices in his head seemed like something from some other time or planet. The faster that he walked the stronger the voices become in his mind. People walked by him cautiously out of their approach to maintain a strategic distance from him. Ezra thought that the people were plotting against him.

To his misfortune, Ezra was having a psychotic breakdown. This bizarre scene happens frequently around the nation. When we hear someone is psychotic, we automatically think of psychopaths and cold-blooded criminals. Inevitably we think they are crazy. And we automatically think of plenty of other myths and misconceptions that only further the stigma surrounding psychosis.

Like a physical health crisis, a mental health crisis can be devastating for individuals, families and communities. While an individual crisis cannot be fully predicted, we can plan how we structure services and organize approaches to best meet the needs of those individuals who experience a mental health crisis. Too often that experience is met with delay, detainment and even denial of service in a manner that creates undue burden on the person, law enforcement, emergency departments and justice systems (National Guidelines for Behavioral Health Crisis Care Best Practice Toolkit, 2020).

Communicating with People Who Are Mentally Ill

In our society, there is a powerful negative stigma attached to mental illness, especially the more severe forms, like schizophrenia. Schizophrenia is a type of psychosis that is generally characterized by hallucinations, disordered thinking, and delusions. Schizophrenia is what Ezra suffered from. Most schizophrenics and others who are mentally ill are no more likely to be dangerous than the general population, but because of their bizarre and unpredictable behavior, they often frighten people.

Popular media fuels stereotypes about mental illness and dangerousness, because that is how they generally are portrayed on the screen. Newspapers sensationalize crimes committed by people with mental illness.

Our fear of mentally-ill people also stems from our own inability to communicate with them and our lack of knowledge about mental illness. Just because they may be behaving in ways that don't make sense to us doesn't mean that we can't provide them with service that is part of our jobs to provide any constituent or customer.

According to (Swink, 2010) the following guidelines for communicating with a person with mental illness:

- Be respectful to the person. When someone feels respected and heard, they are more likely to return respect and consider what you have to say.

- If they are experiencing events like hallucinations, be aware that the hallucinations or the delusions they experience are their reality. You will not be able to talk them out of their reality. They experience their hallucinations or delusional thoughts as real and are motivated by them. Communicate that you understand that they experience those events. Do not pretend that you experience them.

- Some people with paranoia may be frightened, so be aware that they may need more body space than you.

- Do not assume that they are not smart and will believe anything you tell them. Mental illness has nothing to do with a person's intelligence level. So do not lie to them, as it will usually break any rapport you might want to establish.

- Do not just pass them on to another person like a "hot potato" just to get rid of them. This may save you time in the short run but may come back to haunt you later or cause problems for someone else. Anyone who is passed unnecessarily from one person to another can become angry or violent. Refer them to someone else only if it is an appropriate referral.

- Listen to the person and try to understand what he/she is communicating. Often, if you do not turn off your communicating skills, you will be able to understand. Find out what reality-based needs you can meet.
- If needed, set limits with the person as you would others. For example, "I only have five minutes to talk to you" or "If you scream, I will not be able to talk to you."
- Keep a current list of community resources, like shelters, food programs, and mental health services that you can suggest to them (if they need it). Some people will not accept the suggestion, but some will.
- Call for help (police, security, or colleagues) if you feel physically threatened or need help de-escalating the person.

Perhaps the most potent element of all, in an effective crisis service system, is relationships. To be human. To be compassionate. We know from experience that immediate access to help, hope and healing saves lives (National Guidelines for Behavioral Health Crisis Care Best Practice Toolkit, 2020).

Mental Illness and Violence

Mental illness alone does not increase the risk of violence, but when mental illness is combined with other risk factors such as substance abuse, it does increase the risk of violence. Previous research has produced mixed results about the link between mental illness and violence.

In a landmark study conducted by (Elbogen & Johnson, 2009) at the University of North Carolina-Chapel Hill School of Medicine, data were evaluated on nearly 35,000 people. All were interviewed about their mental health, history of violence, and use of substances between 2001 and 2003. They found that the percentage of participants reporting a mental illness reflected the percentages found in the general population and in other studies.

In a second interview conducted in 2004 or 2005, participants were asked about any violent behavior, such as committing a sexual assault, fighting, or setting fires, in the time between interviews. Between the first and second interviews, 2.9% of participants said they had been violent. When Elbogen and Johnson evaluated the possible associations between mental illness, violence, and other factors, having a mental illness alone did not predict violence, but having a mental illness and a substance abuse problem did increase the risk of violence.

When Elbogen and Johnson looked at those who only had a severe mental illness, 2.4% had been violent. But when they looked at those with major depression and substance abuse or dependence, 6.47% had been violent. When they looked at those with schizophrenia, 5.15% reported violent behavior in the time period between the interviews. When a person with schizophrenia also had substance abuse or dependence problems, 12.66% reported violent behavior in the time between the interviews.

The highest risk for violence was found in those who had mental illness, a substance abuse problem, and a history of violence. These participants had 10 times the risk of violence than those who only had mental illness.

Other factors that predicted violent behavior included:

- History of juvenile detention or physical abuse
- Having seen parental fighting
- Recent divorce
- Unemployment
- Being victimized themselves
- Being younger, male, and low-income

Whether a person is mentally ill or not, one does not just "snap" as is often reported in the media. There is generally a progression of behaviors down a pathway toward violence and those behaviors often become noticeable as a person moves down that path.

As public service providers, parents, teachers, friends, family, coworkers, and law enforcers, we should learn how to recognize those behavioral warning signs and communicate our concerns to people who might be able to help. Unfortunately, it can be extremely difficult to get help for someone with mental illness that doesn't accept the help.

Remember that not just the homeless and the poor suffer from mental illness. Mental illness has no racial, economic or intellectual boundaries. You may not be in the business of being a social worker or psychologist. You may be too busy at work to spend a lot of time with any one person, mentally ill or not.

Many people who you may consider "strange" have a right to seek your services and have a real need that you can meet within your job description. Try to limit your interventions to relatively short periods of time, but realize that taking time to try to communicate effectively with the person may save you a lot of time in the long run and help someone in the process.

People with mental illness have many gifts and talents that add to our life as a community of faith. The first step in interacting with people with a mental illness is to recognize that each person has dignity. The next step is to recognize in ourselves any preconceived negative images and prejudices we may have toward people with mental illness. These usually are formed by distorted media images, isolated bad experiences of people with mental illnesses, or the many myths surroundings mental illness. Once we strip away the generalizations and distortions, we are better able to see a person for who they truly are, a person created in the image of God.

People with mental illness should not be defined by the disease they have but by the person they are. When we start labeling people as a disease, we see them as problems rather than a person. So, it is important to separate the illness and symptoms from the person. Each illness carries with its symptoms that may affect how people interact with us and we with them. The intensity and severity of the illness impacts one's ability to communicate. Mental illness can affect a person's ability to think sequentially, to manage emotions or mood swings, and to be in relationship with others.

Someone with depression may seem uninterested or distant. That is a symptom to be recognized but not indicative of the person they are outside the illness. A person with schizophrenia may hear voices or experience hallucinations which are very real to them and their reality. It is important not to deny that they are experiencing those symptoms to learn more about what they are going through. A person who has a panic disorder may be uncomfortable in Church or at meetings, so it is important to be sensitive to the person's need to get up and move around.

In crisis situations, people with a mental illness may exhibit symptoms relative to the intensity of their illness and the treatment they are or are not receiving. A person exhibiting untreated symptoms of mental illness such as severe depression, schizophrenia, or bipolar disease may need crisis intervention by trained professionals. Therefore, it is important to know the resource available in your area to get a person help. We should not engage the person in arguing or confrontation about the symptoms but rather comfort them and calmly help them to seek treatment. We should always act in a safe manner for ourselves and the person we are ministering to.

You may not be a psychotherapist who treats the symptoms of mental illness just as you may not be an oncologist who discusses remedies for a cancer. Yet, you can act as a spiritual friend and companion who journeys in faith with those who are in need or suffering and often isolated by their illness. In the recovery model, we are part of the social and/or spiritual component in a person's life. Understanding the symptoms of the mental illness will help us to better communicate, minister, advocate, and pray with people with mental illness.

Listening is an important part of interacting with people with mental illness. People's personal stories are sacred. A person's story of suffering, coping with a life changing illness can be frightening and lonely experiences. Often a major mental illness is accompanied by doubts about God and can cause a crisis of faith. Holy listening, that is, listening in the context of the healing presence of God, means hearing what a person tells us and letting their story unfold.

We respond and react to their story in a non-judgmental way with unconditional love or the person. Holy listening allows and may often encourage people to relate their experiences in a support atmosphere that leads to comfort and healing. Holy listening brings one to a richer understanding of God's unconditional love for us through our acceptance of one another. It also may lead to a mutuality of understanding that allows the person who is ministering to another to begin to see that they are being ministered to as well. This supportive process leads to solidarity and mutuality that enriches faith and hope. The listener then becomes the learner, and both journey the path to wholeness and holiness.

As individuals and as church we are called to create an environment that sends a message of acceptance that encourages people to tell their story. Such an environment in fact gives a person permission to tell their story, which they may otherwise feel too uncomfortable or too embarrassed or to stigmatized to tell. This process usually develops over a significant period. We need to patiently allow the story to unfold.

Mental health is a growing concern in this country. Illnesses such as depression, bipolar disorder, and schizophrenia affect more than 43 million Americans. Only a small percentage will seek out professional help to challenge their demons (Mental Health By the Numbers, 2019). The proof is right there and yet a majority of people still scoff at those less fortunate than they are. They laugh at the girl sitting by herself. They tease the boy who can't adjust easily. They avoid the homeless person who is trying to stay alive. They judge. That's all we know how to do in this country. Judge. Look at someone, make assumptions based off stereotypes, and decide that everything we think is 100% accurate.

The problem is, we don't know what anyone else is going through. Often, we don't even know what our best friend, cousin, brother, or mother is going through. Even if we did, their description and emotions would be concepts we just can't grasp. Mental illnesses doesn't discriminate based on socioeconomic status, gender or race. It can befall anyone, for any reason, at any time. They may hide it in the belief that society thinks they don't matter. Society may say they are weird, crazy, odd, quiet, not normal. We judge so much that they are unable to beat what seems inevitable to some of them (Bryant, 2018).

You can't always see mental illness, but that does not mean it does not have a face. Change your attitudes toward others around you. A smile of understanding may help save the depression on their face. Without question, being a Black female and growing up in the 1960s (where we had way more to deal with than mental health conditions), mental health was never really discussed. Relentless stigma accompanies mental health conditions. From the words we use—like "crazy," "cray cray," "psycho," "nuts"—to hurtful jokes about people who live with mental health conditions, stigma surrounding mental health in my culture is deeply rooted. But there is no shame in having a mental health condition. The true shame is not getting the treatment you need to have a good life.

On this account, African-Americans need to know that a mental health condition is no different than a physical one. Our brains are the most important organ in our bodies and can get sick just like our hearts, lungs, and livers. Not only that, you can recover from a mental health condition and lead a healthy life. Further, African-Americans are not immune from mental health conditions, and 5.6% of us die by suicide. Up to about two million (10%) African-American men live with depression (Bryant, 2018).

The religious community has much work to do to address the shame, guilt and stigma associated with mental illness. Unfortunately, very few seminaries incorporate adequate information about mental illness into their core curriculum. Studies show that a majority of individuals with a mental health issues go first to a spiritual leader for help. Yet, clergy are often the least effective in providing appropriate support and referral information.

African Americans are much more likely to rely on their faith as a coping mechanism for dealing with depression and anxiety than to utilize a mental health professional (Armstrong, 2019). Social stigmas surrounding mental health along with the historical and socioeconomic impacts of slavery, impact the narrative surrounding mental health in African American churches. Such statements as: "You're not relying on God enough," "You aren't praying enough," and "God is the only answer," may infer that to seek help outside of the church equals a lack of faith.

Ayana Therapy (2020) recommends the Black church practice the following responsibilities in relation to mental health:

- Teach the church community that mental illness exists and is valid. Mental health conditions exist as much as physical health conditions and can even be directly correlated to physical circumstances. Once it is recognized that mental health awareness is valuable to spiritual wellness, there can be true restorative justice between communities.

- Refrain from how the church and its leaders view and address mental health. Individuals can have faith, seek therapy, and even take necessary medications simultaneously. Changing the narrative behind mental illness within the church de-stigmatizes the conversation.

- Effectively training church leaders and staff to recognize mental health issues. As spiritual counselors and advisers recognizing the signs of anxiety, depression, and other mental illnesses can assist with truly understanding the demographic they serve.

- Pursue potential mental health partners. Being able to create a cultural climate that focuses on the restoration of religion and mental health can offer healing within generations of black families.

Our deep-rooted religious beliefs go all the way back to slavery when religion was the one solid foundation we had during those times. Our ancestors then—like we African-Americans now—lived with depression, anxiety, bipolar and Post Traumatic Stress Disorder but, back then, there weren't any names for those conditions. Back then, people who battled a mental health condition were simply locked up, wandered the streets, or even put to death (Bryant, 2018).

With all that my culture had to deal with throughout history, present-day African Americans feel we don't need help mentally. All we need to do today is the same our ancestors did, which is: "Pray about it. Give it to God." But you wouldn't tell someone with cancer, diabetes or heart problem to just pray about it or give it to God, would you? You'd hopefully say: "You need to see a doctor." But when it comes to mental health in the African-American community, there is very little compassion or empathy.

Don't get me wrong, there's nothing wrong with praying for recovery from a mental health condition, but we still have to be proactive. We can't "pray away" a mental health condition. We have to get help.

Kimberly Lived Experience of System Failure

From my personal and professional experience, the over diagnosis of schizophrenia in African Americans has led to inappropriate treatment, including excessive use of anti-psychotics, excessive dosing, and under prescribing mood stabilizers. The result is suboptimal care and poorer outcomes for blacks. Subsequently, not all symptoms and problems in life are caused by mental disorders, and mislabeling can be extremely harmful to those labeled falsely. In my opinion, it is always much safer and more accurate to *under* diagnose than to *over* diagnose. It is easy enough to add a diagnosis when time and experience prove it to be appropriate, but once a misdiagnosis is made, it takes on a life of its own and is extremely hard to unmake.

Primarily, the relationship comes first. An accurate diagnosis comes from a collaborative effort with a patient. Moreover, when a person comes in for their first counseling session, it is likely that you are meeting them on one of the worst days of their life. People often wait until their suffering is so desperate that it finally outweighs the fear, mistrust, or embarrassment that previously prevented them from seeking help. Make the search for the diagnosis a joint project that displays your cultural empathy and not implicit bias that feels invasive. The patient should walk out feeling both understood and enlightened. Never forget that this evaluation may be a crucial tipping point that can change the patient's entire future.

Unquestionably, the stigmas of racial inferiority may also adversely affect the treatment of African Americans in the mental health system. Black clinicians have long argued that popular misconceptions, inaccuracies, and stereotypes of the psychology of African Americans could lead to the misdiagnosis of black patients. Current research supports, that over diagnosis of schizophrenia and the under diagnosis of affective disorders are the most frequent types of misdiagnoses for Blacks. The differential interpretation of similar symptoms due to conscious or unconscious acceptance of negative stereotypes of blacks may be a contributing factor to misdiagnosis. Some evidence suggest that the misdiagnosis of black patients persists even when formal diagnostic criteria are utilized.

Thyroid Hormones and Schizophrenia

My sister Kimberly was diagnosed with Grave's disease when she was in her mid-twenties. As a direct result, she soon was diagnosed with hyperthyroidism. There is proven evidence from clinical literature of a close relationship between the severity of hyperthyroidism symptoms (mood swings, nervousness, hyperactivity, irritability, tenseness, difficulty sleeping, short temper, impatience, panic attacks) and the severity of mental health conditions.

Hyperthyroidism is a condition of the thyroid. The thyroid is a small, butterfly-shaped gland located at the front of your neck. It produces tetraiodothyronine (T4) and triiodothyronine (T3), which are two primary hormones that control how your cells use energy. Your thyroid gland regulates your metabolism through the release of these hormones. Hyperthyroidism occurs when the thyroid makes too much T4, T3, or both.

Grave's disease, an autoimmune disorder, is the most common cause of hyperthyroidism. It causes antibodies to stimulate the thyroid to secrete too much hormone. Grave's disease occurs more often in women than in men. Grave's disease and hyperthyroidism share many of the same symptoms. Kimberly experienced multiple debilitating symptoms including an increase in appetite, unprovoked change in taste, weight changes, increase in thirst, change in menstrual cycle, and abnormal protrusion of eyes that bulged from the eye sockets, enlarged thyroid (goiter), and hair loss.

She would often become very agitated and emotionally explosive, crying, and raging about things she could ordinarily handle with ease. She would start arguments with myself and others over relatively insignificant issues. Moreover, the rapid changes in her hormone levels that she constantly experienced were unsettling.

Kimberly had been taking synthetic thyroid hormones for decades. The synthetic thyroid hormones (man-made thyroid hormones) worked to raise abnormally low levels of natural thyroid hormones in her body. She was hopeful that the therapy would decrease the growth of the unsightly enlarged goiter that disfigured her neck. Above all, she truly wished that the effect of the therapy would reduce the abnormal protrusion of her eyes, which she was extremely embarrassed about. She couldn't even take two steps out of the house without an onslaught of cruel jokes from what seemed like the whole neighborhood. Kids, and adults make fun at things they don't understand. When it comes to mental illness, lack of understanding, which often proceeds lack of compassion, isn't uncommon within our community (Snyder, 2020).

When going to the doctor for lab work, the reports would reflect extremely low levels of thyroid-stimulating hormone in her blood. According to the doctor, the low level of thyroid-stimulating hormone (TSH) was responsible for her erratic behavior.

Kimberly grew tired of the taking the medications and stopped taking them. She would complain that the physiological side effects were like the symptoms of the disease itself. According to her, the medicine caused her to feel depressed, anxious, and to have mood swings. An unfortunate set of circumstances led to what I believe was a misdiagnosis of psychiatric symptoms. Which woefully resulted to a diagnosis of schizophrenia.

According to the (DSM 5), the definition of Schizophrenia is a severe and chronic mental disorder characterized by disturbances in thought, perception, and behavior. Schizophrenia involves a range of cognitive, behavioral, and emotional symptoms, and it can be difficult to diagnose. There is no simple physical or lab test for schizophrenia, and diagnosis involves the recognition of a constellation of symptoms negatively impacting social or occupational functioning.

The psychotic features of the disorder typically emerge between the mid-teens and mid-thirties, with the peak age of onset of the first psychotic episode in the early to mid-twenties for males and late twenties for females.

Diagnosis Criteria

The DSM-5 outlines the following criterion to make a diagnosis of schizophrenia:

Two or more of the following for at least a one-month (or longer) period of time, and at least one of them must be 1, 2, or 3:
- Delusions
- Hallucinations
- Disorganized speech
- Grossly disorganized or catatonic behavior
- Negative symptoms, such as diminished emotional expression
- Impairment in one of the major areas of functioning for a significant period of time since the onset of the disturbance: work, interpersonal relations, or self-care.

Some signs of the disorder must last for a continuous period of at least six months. This six-month period must include at least one month of symptoms (or less if treated) that meet criterion A (active phase symptoms) and may include periods of residual symptoms. During residual periods, only negative symptoms may be present. Schizoaffective disorder and bipolar or depressive disorder with psychotic features have been ruled out: No major depressive or manic episodes occurred concurrently with active phase symptoms. If mood episodes (depressive or manic) have occurred during active phase symptoms, they have been present for a minority of the total duration of the active and residual phases of the illness. The disturbance is not caused by the effects of a substance or another medical condition.

Associated Features

There are a number of symptoms that contribute to a diagnosis of schizophrenia.

- Inappropriate affect (laughing in the absence of a stimulus)
- Disturbed sleep pattern
- Dysphoric mood (can be depression, anxiety, or anger)
- Anxiety and phobias
- Depersonalization (detachment, feeling of disconnect)
- Derealization (a feeling that surrounding aren't real)

- Cognitive deficits impacting language, processing, executive function, and/or memory
- Lack of insight into disorder
- Social cognition deficits
- Hostility and aggression

Cognitive impairments caused by the disorder may persist when other symptoms are in remission. This contributes to impairments in functioning in employment, interpersonal relationships, and the ability to engage in proper self-care.

Suicide Risk

Research by Hor and Taylor (2010) supports... 5% to 6% of people with schizophrenia die by suicide. Nearly 20% make suicide attempts on more than one occasion, and many more have significant suicidal thoughts. Suicidal behavior can be in response to hallucinations and suicide risk remains high over the lifespan of individuals with schizophrenia.

Functional Consequences

Schizophrenia is associated with social and occupational dysfunction. Completing education and maintaining employment are negatively impacted by symptoms of the illness, and most individuals diagnosed with schizophrenia are employed at a lower level than their parents. Many have few or limited social relationships outside of their immediate family.

I deeply believe that Kimberly never met the (DSM-5) criteria for schizophrenia. It is my clinical opinion that the diagnosis was incorrect given that the true criteria in the (DSM-5), and the providers who made the diagnosis may not have taken into consideration the debilitating effects of hyperthyroidism and Grave's disease.

Unfortunately, my beloved sister became a frequent visitor to psychiatric hospitals while under the influence of psychotropic medication paired with impaired cognitive abilities. It is distressing that the mental health and medical system appears to have failed my sister. Undoubtedly, Kimberly's psychiatric illness was acutely exacerbated by Hyperthyroidism due to Grave's disease.

Indubitably, at the prime age of 54, my sister Kimberly ended her life by suicide. Regrettably, she had never shared with our family any thoughts of harming herself. Yet, what went wrong? She seemed to have had her life in order. My parents raised her in the church. She was from a good home.

Kimberly wasn't "all right" emotionally, psychologically, nor spiritually. She had been baptized at an early age and carried the Lord in her heart. She graduated from high school in Grand Rapids, Michigan and attended college in nearby Kalamazoo. Later, Kimberly worked in the health care industry as a Certified Nursing Assistant (CNA) for many years until her health no longer permitted. She was a hard worker and put her heart into any job that she performed.

Kimberly was a warm and loving woman who enjoyed laughing, smiling, and singing with and for family and friends. She was an exceptional artist and loved to sketch in her spare time as well as keep active through walking, crossword puzzle, and reading. Kimberly was also a God-fearing woman who enjoyed being active in her church.

Within her heart, however, was the simple love of being with her family, especially her nieces and nephews. Kimberly loved to watch classic television shows and movies. She was warm, generous, and loving, and would help anyone that needed her assistance. She would often send letters to her family and loved to write on beautiful stationary. Kimberly also enjoyed shopping and often loved to wear beautiful and unique hats.

She dreamed of visiting Los Angeles, California and walking along the shoreline. Kimberly was literally hiding in the church. Few people at church or in her minuscule social circle knew about her debilitating depression and repeated hospitalizations. They were not aware that she was misdiagnosed with paranoid schizophrenia. For two years she suffered in silence, hiding in plain sight.

God wants to use Kimberly's story for His glory. He desired to take her weaknesses and turn them into strengths for our family and for the rest of the body of Christ. If our family pretends like nothing happened and continues to keep her death by suicide a secret, how will anyone else be helped by her experiences?

The Link Between Schizophrenia and Hypothyroidism

Schizophrenia is a devastating mental disorder that affects 1% of adults worldwide. In very severe cases, positive thought disorder manifests as unintelligible speech...of the speech produced by schizophrenia patients suggested that it was more...lead to the language abnormalities, Kuperberg G. R. (2010).

A population-based cross-sectional study was conducted using data retrieved from the largest medical records database in Israel, the Clalit Health Services (CHS). Patients were defined as having hypothyroidism or schizophrenia when there was at least one such documented diagnosis in their medical records. The proportion of schizophrenia was compared between hypothyroid and age- and sex frequency-matched healthy controls. A logistic regression model was used to estimate the association between psychiatric manifestations and hypothyroidism in a multivariate analysis adjusted for age, gender, and smoking status.

The study included 40,843 patients with hypothyroidism and 40,918 age- and sex frequency-matched controls. The proportion of schizophrenia in hypothyroid patients was higher than that in controls (2.01% vs. 1.25%, respectively, $p < 0.0001$). Multivariate logistic regression demonstrated a robust independent association between hypothyroidism and schizophrenia (OR 1.62, $p \leq 0.001$).

Their study confirmed a higher proportion of hypothyroidism among patients with schizophrenia. The awareness of such interrelation should drive physicians treating patients with schizophrenia to consider screening for hypothyroidism. Further studies are required to elucidate the underlying mechanism or the common denominator favoring the co-occurrence of schizophrenia and hypothyroidism (Sharif, et al., 2005).

Moreover, misdiagnosing African Americans with schizophrenia is all to common. A new study from Rutgers University found, African Americans with severe depression are more likely to be misdiagnosed as having schizophrenia than white patients, the finding builds on years of evidence that clinicians' racial biases — whether conscious or unconscious — affect the types of mental-health diagnoses African American are given.

Furthermore, all too often, I've seen common, minor transgressions (like roasting) of school-aged black children be misinterpreted as hostility or aggression. Mistaken cultural nuance is one of the main factors in misdiagnosis of Black people, and this trend is why a lot of Black people have reservations about getting mental health treatment (Snyder, 2020).

To someone that is not of the culture or at least knowledgeable of the culture, it is easy to misconstrue this black teenager's behavior as something much more severe, like ODD. Kids with ODD are typically less playful, more disorderly, spiteful, and argumentative than this boy was. He just talked entirely too much and was seeking attention. It is typical for teenage black boys to laugh at and crack jokes on one another to gain popularity in school settings.

The therapist assigned to treat the boy, a white, middle-age woman, diagnosed his with oppositional defiant disorder (ODD), which is a disorder characterized by hostile, rebellious, and vindictive behavior. Granted, everyone agreed that he had behavioral problems, yet, it's still a clear misinterpretation to perceive roasting as meeting the criteria for ODD.

The child was a high school freshman, and a known "class clown," who obnoxiously "flamed" or "roasted" his classmates (and the teacher) daily, which led to several schoolyard fights and suspensions.

I've known colleagues to misdiagnose black children because they misread cultural behaviors. One of my earliest experiences with misdiagnosis involved an African-American teen who was referred by his school to the agency I was working with to get treatment for insubordination.

Which means they probably don't understand African-American social dynamics. Counselors that are not knowledgeable about black culture many not sufficiently understand specific problems, or even simple commonalities that are unique to the black community.

Misdiagnosis is a significant barrier to mental health treatment for black and brown people. Of course, therapist, just as almost any other professionals, sometimes get diagnosis wrong. Due to our minority status, it's likely, the people we go to for help (doctors, lawyers, psychologist, etc.) are from a different cultural background.

I have learned over the years that when one's mind is made up, this diminishes fear; knowing what must be done does away with fear.
Rosa Parks

Trust in the Lord with all your heart, and do not lean on your own understanding. In all your ways acknowledge him, and he will make straight your paths.
Proverbs 3:5-6

Chapter 3
The Black Church: A Change Agent

The term Black Church is classically defined as the collection of seven major historically Black denominations of the Christian faith in the United States (Lincoln & Mamiya, 1990).
- The National Baptist Convention of America (NBCA)
- The Church of God in Christ (COGIC)
- African Methodist Episcopal (AME) Church
- African Methodist Episcopal Zion (AMEZ) Church
- Methodist Episcopal Church
- National Baptist Convention USA, Inc. (NBA)
- Progressive National Baptist Convention (PNBC).

These denominations encompass approximately 65,000-75,000 churches in the United States, with an estimated membership of 24 million.

According to Pew Research Center's Religious Landscape Study (2014), nearly 8-in-10 Black Americans (79%) identify as Christian. By comparison, 7-in-10 Americans overall (71%) say they are Christian, including 70% of whites, 77% of Latinos and just 34% of Asian Americans. Meanwhile, about 7-in-10 Blacks are Protestant, compared with less than half of the public overall (47%), including 48% of Whites, roughly a quarter of Latinos and 17% of Asian Americans.

One in four families sitting in the pews has a member dealing with mental illness. Yet our religious communities are often silent when it comes to understanding mental disorders as treatable illnesses. Persons struggling with a mental illness and their family members often become detached from their faith communities and their spirituality, which could be an important source of healing, wholeness and hope in times of personal darkness.

Religious views separate blacks from seeking treatment. Our culture is notorious for replacing therapy with prayer. When problems arise, many religious folk rely on scripture to see them through. By no means, am I bashing anyone's beliefs; spirituality can be instrumental in getting through tough times. However, even a prayer from Bishop T.D. Jakes, himself, can't replace treatment from a trained therapist. I hate to say it, but you can't just pray away a mental aliment, like PTSD, no more than you can pray away a broken leg (Snyder, 2020).

Conversations about mental health is important, especially for communities of color and the faith community who supports people of color because it is such a taboo topic. It is also critical to have realistic conversation about healthy ways to seek socio-psychological and emotional support versus using destructive patterns including abuse, suicide, cannabis/marijuana use, alcohol, and other destructive behavior to cope.

Traditional societal stigma surrounding mental health has even more of an impact when it comes to communities who were once legally prohibited from seeking mental and emotional health support; and when they did, it often led to extreme punitive results. As a result, most people of color turned to the Black church to help them spiritually focus on addressing issues of depression, suicide, trauma, grief, etc. This has not proven to be sufficient. Although the spiritual component is critical, it is equally critical to acknowledge that an individual may need to seek assistance from mental health professionals and counselors to be whole mentally, spiritually, physically, and emotionally.

There is a great need to spread the word that mental illness occurs among men and women of all ages, that it crosses all racial, ethnic and religious lines, and that it occurs at all economic levels of society. The general public needs to be more aware of the facts about mental illness. The stigma surrounding them must be erased so that individuals and families are comfortable seeking help just as they would for a physical illness.

As a means to educate the public and to reduce mental health stigma (specifically among urban African American congregations) Emerging HOPE Ministries was formed. The grass-roots program began in 2017 and is founded and co-directed by the author with her husband. The team hosts annual Mental Health Forums to provide a place where the individuals, groups, and organizations can come together in Kalamazoo, Michigan. The participants share information and ideas with other interested professionals, the public, and the media on the importance of spreading the word that mental illness is an epidemic. Those invited are encouraged to work together to do whatever possible to eradicate the stigma associated with it.

There are a plethora of mental health service providers and many community outreach events pertaining to mental health wellness available to individuals with mental health challenges. However, studies have shown that many African Americans seek mental health help from their church and few of the outreach services adequately represented the African American community. According to Crabb (1997), many people who are reluctant to talk with a professional may feel more comfortable being a part of a church ministry that meets their need. Individuals often will trust those they feel are accountable to God before they will trust professionals who may not. More should be learned about differences in need according to location, social standing, and cultural orientation so as to identify treatments and programs that are especially beneficial to African Americans.

Thus, (Milstein, et al., 2008) developed The Clergy Outreach Professional Engagement Mannequin (COPE) with a specific mission that labored to examine the relationship between clergy and parishioners living with mental illness. They utilize a dictation of religion-inclusive burden reduction through by dividing resources. For instance, clergy may speak in conformity with a therapist in regards to one of his or her parishioners. In turn, psychologists utilize their expertise; together with viable venues in conformity with pray associative aid, then mean-structured activities.

This mannequin additionally includes a system with the aid of clergy, then psychologists, present forums regarding a range of matters. For instance, psychologists would possibly assign a conference about despair while ministers speak regarding the purposes concerning Bible study then Sunday faculty activities. This kind about intervention looks to correctly tackle the problems promoted within preceding clergy counseling practices.

Moreover, Emerging HOPE Ministries conducts Mental Health Forums to foster dialogue among a broad range of stakeholders—practitioners, policymakers, community members, recipients of services, and others—and provide ongoing opportunities to confront issues of African American and disenfranchised individual centered around mental health disparities. Likewise, the Forum provides a neutral venue for broad-ranging discussions that aide in coordination and cooperation between public, faith-based, service recipients, and private stakeholders to eradicate the stigma of mental illness, specifically among people of African American and disenfranchised populations.

Clergy Attitudes Have Significant Influence on Their Parishioners

African American clergy are a primary source of mental health care for socioeconomically diverse Black adults and are trusted gatekeepers for referral to mental health specialist. Resources suggest, approximately 50% of African Americans use only one source of mental healthcare obtained help from clergy providers. A comprehensive analysis of African American clergy in a Kalamazoo, Michigan revealed that clergy averaged more than six hours of counseling work each week and often addressed serious problems similar to those seen by secular mental health professionals (Emerging HOPE Ministries, 2017).

In one study, clergy reported that they spent a minimum of 15% of their pastoral time doing counseling with their parishioners. This percentage was even higher in rural areas where there are fewer social resources and community mental health centers (Blank et al., 2002). However, the extent and nature of the counseling services are dependent upon the perceptions, beliefs, and skills of the clergy themselves.

There is a sector within the black church community known as "prayer warriors." Prayer warriors are highly trained spiritual people who are committed to praying for others. If you know church folks, you have heard people call on the prayer warriors to help them during trying times.

I think was all have seem a social media post or two (or a hundred) saying, "I need all my prayer warriors to help me out on this one . . ." Or a simple "pray for me" without giving any details as to what we're praying for. I can't help but wonder how many of those calls for prayer were related to problems best suited for a therapist. If I were a betting man, I'd say a lot (Synder, 2020).

For instance, one survey of ministers indicated that they frequently use scripture and spiritual advice as a part of their counseling sessions. Some reported that they believed emotional problems were caused by unsatisfactory relationship with God. But, more reported that these problems were due to life stressors. Clergy who were more educated were more likely to have referred to a psychological professional (Mattis, 2007). Still, it is important to note, parishioners are usually the ones who seek therapy, and they reported that they were uncomfortable talking about some types of problems with clergy (Young et al., 2003).

Factors affecting a parishioner's desire to consult clergy included: character of the clergy, previous relationship, perceived competence, and shame or uneasiness about an issue. They felt comfortable talking about issues regarding money, bereavement, family or life problems. They also frequently went to clergy to talk about emotional issues or major life decisions. On the other hand, churchgoers reported apprehension about talking to pastors about sex, drugs, domestic violence, and other more sensitive issues.

Clergy and Mental Health Professionals are Trained Differently

Clergy noted that they could use more training with certain types of issues, as well as locating social resources to pass along to their members (Neighbors, Musick, & Williams, 1998). Kloos et al. (1995) found that clergy said they needed training in psychological issues, and that they sometimes had difficulty deciding when to refer their parishioners to psychological professionals (Mattis,2007; Neighbors et al., 1998; Young et al., 2003).

For these types of issues, churches and clergy need psychologists to act as community advocates, consultants, program evaluators, and other roles. Conversely, clergy can offer a wide range of expertise to psychologists, including specific ways to address personal needs and an enriched understanding of religious issues and how they are lived out in the lives of churchgoers.

Clergy and psychologists Collaboration are Important

A study (McMinn et al. 1998) reviewed a group that comprised both disciplines. They discovered that 80% of those surveyed indicated that it was important to consider religion in therapy. However, very few psychologists reported actually using religion in therapy, and very few clergy reported using psychological resources in their counseling. It seems that there is a recognized need, but few people often act on this need. In their perceptions of what would facilitate collaboration, professionals from both disciplines noted shared beliefs, shared information, and mutual respect as key factors.

It is important to note that the concept of "shared beliefs" does not mean denominational or doctrinal agreement, but shared beliefs about the connection between psychological and spiritual issues. Previous research indicates that clergy level of education, prior pastoral training, size of the church, and other variables impact referral and counseling practices of clergy. A survey by Blasi, Husaini, and Drumwright (1998) found that pastors who were more educated and those who were full-time pastors were more likely to refer their parishioners to specialists (mental health or medical) for help with specific problems.

The challenge with all the articles reviewed (which examine clergy behaviors and attitudes) is that they use qualitative interview data, with questions developed independently by each set of researchers. Therefore, there is little reliability across studies, and we are unaware of the exact questions being asked. However, since there is extraordinarily little research available in the field, the less sophisticated exploratory research is as necessary as it is incomplete. On the other hand, the data examining service seeking behaviors in African Americans is based on large scale census-like data sets using statistical analyses. These data are much more generalizable to the larger population and give a better estimation of the actual rates of service seeking and attitudes toward mental health.

While spirituality is the forefront of pastoral counseling, it is the background in traditional therapy, even if it is inclusive of religious/spiritual issues. Psychologists who seek to collaborate with clergy must keep in mind the distinction that should be made between psychotherapy and pastoral care. Pastoral care can be described as "supportive" rather than therapeutic in many cases. For people who may need to simply talk through a specific problem, or are seeking reassurance from a trusted authority, it is perfectly suitable in order to address the symptoms or problem currently being faced.

Often, the fact that these supportive conversations can take place in a familiar setting makes them more effective than traditional psychotherapy might be. Wiley (1991) describes the African American church as "a caring community" in which there is an inherent support system against oppression and struggle. She argues that this system should help people work toward spiritual and emotional freedom.

This system is holistic in nature and seeks to address mental, emotional, sociological and economic needs. This kind of support provides a wonderful foundation for clergy to begin the process of healing in the church community. However, clergy recognize that there are some problems that cannot be tackled purely within the context of the church. As such, an important function of pastoral care is referral (Richardson, 1989), and this function is what makes clergy attitudes and relationships with mental health professionals so important.

Historically, the Black church, a heterogeneous consortium of establishments has served the spiritual, social, economic, and political needs of its members. African American culture has multiple elements of the church woven into its fabric. The most extensive involvement in the delivery of social service programs is provided by the African American church, including counseling (Blank et al. 2002). Furthermore, findings indicate that Black religious congregations may be more willing and ready to engage in collaborative efforts with mental health providers (Young et al 2003). However, church-based programs are at fledgling stage of development, specifically those geared toward mental disorders among African Americans (Robinson 2017).

Pastoral support for faith-based mental health services can go a long way toward destigmatizing psychological services. Recruiting the lead pastor as the key figure in support of the health program is a key factor in successfully establishing and sustaining these initiatives in black churches (Campbell et al. 2007). Increasing mental health care among African Americans is a complex issue for which there is no single solution.

I stress that the Black church has a major role in mental health service provision, yet the current literature on church-based mental healthcare is extremely limited. Further effort, in particular that which utilizes participatory approaches, is needed to delve into opportunities and limitations of church based mental health care for African Americans.

> Clergy who were more educated were more likely to have referred to a psychological professional (Mattis, 2007). Still, it is important to note, parishioners are usually the ones who seek therapy, and they reported that they were uncomfortable talking about some types of problems with clergy (Young et al., 2003).

There is never time in the future in which we will work out our salvation. The challenge is in the moment; the time is always now.
James Baldwin, author

Chapter 4
Facing Unique Challenges

African Americans take up a distinctive place in the history of America and in contemporary national life. The legacy of slavery and discrimination continues to influence their social and economic standing. The mental health of African Americans can be appreciated only within this wider historical context. Resilience and forging of social ties have enabled many African Americans to overcome adversity and to maintain a high degree of mental health.

Approximately 12% of people in the United States, or 34 million, identify themselves as African American (U.S. Census Bureau, 2001a). However, this figure may be lower than the actual number because African Americans are overrepresented among people who are hard to reach through the census, such as the homeless or incarcerated (O'Hare et al., 1991). Census takers especially miss younger and middle-aged African American males because they are overrepresented in these vulnerable populations and because they often decline to participate in the census (Williams & Jackson, 2000).

The African American population is increasing in diversity as greater numbers of immigrants arrive from Africa and the Caribbean. Indeed, 6% of all Blacks in the United States today are foreign-born. Most of them come from the Caribbean, especially the Dominican Republic, Haiti, and Jamaica. In 1998, nearly 1.5 million Blacks residing in the United States were born in the Caribbean (U.S. Census, 1998). In addition, since 1983, more than 100,000 refugees have come to the United States from African nations.

According to Holden et al., 2014, despite decades of research, recognition and treatment of mental illness and its comorbidities still remain a significant public health problem in the United States. Ethnic minorities are identified as a population that is vulnerable to mental health disparities and face unique challenges pertaining to mental health care. Psychiatric illness is associated with great physical, emotional, functional, and societal burden.

The primary health care setting may be a promising venue for screening, assessment, and treatment of mental illnesses for ethnic minority populations. We propose a comprehensive, innovative, culturally centered integrated care model to address the complexities within the health care system, from the individual level (which includes provider and patient factors), to the system level (which includes practice culture and system functionality issues.)

Our multidisciplinary investigative team acknowledges the importance of providing culturally-tailored integrative health care to holistically concentrate on physical, mental, emotional, and behavioral problems among ethnic minorities in a primary care setting. It is our intention that the proposed model will be useful for health practitioners, contribute to the reduction of mental health disparities, and promote better mental health and well-being for ethnic minority individuals, families, and communities. Major depression is one of the most common mental health problems in the United States. It affects approximately 14.8 million adults, with women ages 18 to 45 years old accounting for the largest proportion of functional impairment of this group (Substance Abuse and Mental Health Service Administration (SAMHSA, 2010).

Past adversity, which included slavery, sharecropping, and race-based exclusion from health, educational, social, and economic resources, converts into the socioeconomic disparities experienced by African Americans today. Socioeconomic status, in turn, is linked to mental health. Poor mental health is more common among those who are impoverished than among those who are more affluent. Likewise, socioeconomic disparities increases likelihood of African Americans becoming members of high-need populations, such as the homeless, incarcerated, substance abusers, and children in foster care; particularly due to a parent who is victim to these issues.

The Epidemiologic Catchment Area study (ECA) of the 1980s sampled residents of Baltimore, St. Louis, Durham-Piedmont, Los Angeles, and New Haven. They assessed samples from both the community at large and institutions such as mental hospitals, jails, residential drug or alcohol treatment facilities, and nursing homes (Robins & Regier, 1991). In total, it included 4,638 African Americans, 12,944 Whites, and 1,600 Hispanics. A more recent study, the National Comorbidity Survey (NCS), included a representative sample of persons living in the community that included 666 African Americans, 4,498 Whites, and 713 additional U.S. residents (Kessler et al., 1994). Participants of both studies reported whether or not they had experienced symptoms of frequently diagnosed mental disorders in the past month, the past year, or at any time during their lives.

In light of the findings, whether African Americans differ from Whites in rate of mental illness cannot be answered simply. On the ECA, African Americans had higher levels of any lifetime or current disorder than Whites. This was true both over the respondent's lifetime (Robins & Regier, 1991) and over the past month (Regier et. al., 1993). Taking into account differences in age, gender, marital status, and socioeconomic status, however, the Black-White difference was eliminated. From the ECA then, it appears that African Americans in the community suffer from higher rates of mental illness than Whites, but that the difference is explained by differences in demographic composition of the groups and in their social positions.

Evidence from the NCS, on the other hand, indicated that even without controlling for demographic and socioeconomic differences, African Americans living in the community had lower lifetime prevalence of mental illness than did White Americans living in the community (Kessler et al., 1996). At least one point seems to be converged from the results of these major epidemiological surveys: The rates of mental illness among African Americans are similar to those of Whites.

Yet this judgment, too, is open to challenge because of African American over-representation in high-need populations. Persons who live, for example, in psychiatric hospitals, prisons, the inner city, and poor rural areas are not readily accessible to researchers who conduct household surveys. By counting members of these high-need groups, higher rates of mental illness among African Americans might be detected.

A study discussed in the Surgeon General's report on mental health (DHHS, 1999) included an assessment of how much mental health care children in four geographic regions received. Children were identified as having an unfulfilled need if they were impaired because of mental illness and had zero mental health care in the preceding six months. African American children and youth were more likely to fall into this category than were White children and youth (Shaffer et al., 1996).

A 10-year-old African American male, "John," suffered from declining grades. Formerly a B and C student, he now received Ds. His mother could not explain his drop in academic achievement. John was unable to concentrate on homework and was sick to his stomach whenever he studied. When questioned, John said that his father, now deceased, had formerly helped him carry out his assignments.

John told this story of his father's death: He and his father had been entering an elevator. They came upon two men arguing; one drew a gun and began to shoot. John's father, an innocent bystander, was shot in the stomach. He died on the moving elevator. The shooting and death produced a nauseating smell; John became sick and threw up.

Studying reminded John of his father's death and triggered nausea. This recognition helped to guide treatment. The focus was on providing a supportive relationship in which John could grieve his father's death. Overwhelmed, his mother had been unable to tolerate the grief. Over time, John was able to transform his remorse into academic effort as a memorial to his father. His grades gradually improved. (Bell, 1997).

Little is known about rates of mental disorders among older African Americans. Older African American ECA respondents exhibited higher rates of cognitive impairment than did their counterparts from other groups. The rate of severe cognitive impairment continued to be higher for African Americans even after the researchers controlled for differences in demographic factors and socioeconomic status. Cognitive impairment is strongly related to education; simple measures may fail to assess fully the long-term impact of excluding African Americans from good schools.

Even less is known about the mental health of older African Americans whose physical health is poor. It appears that many living in nursing homes need psychiatric care (Class et al., 1996). In addition, 27 percent of older African Americans living in public housing needed mental health treatment (Black et al., 1997). Several studies have examined rates of depressive symptoms in older African Americans living in the community. Three of the more rigorous research efforts reported few differences in depressive symptoms between African Americans and Caucasians (Husaini, 1997, Blazer et al., 1998; Gallo et al., 1998.) As with older Caucasians, elevated symptoms of depression in African Americans have been related to health problems (Okwumabua et al., 1997; Mui & Burnette, 1994).

Sometimes symptoms are considered not as markers of an underlying mental disorder but as mental health problems in their own right. Although much remains to be learned about symptom distress, it can pose significant problems. Symptoms of depression have been associated with considerable impairment in the performance of day-to-day tasks of living, comparable to that associated with common medical conditions (Wells et al., 1989). Among African Americans especially, symptoms of depression are associated with increased risk of hypertension (Pickering, 2000).

A 17-year-old African American male in foster care, "Michael," was referred for mental health care. He was described as "hostile." He had recently dropped out of school. Michael was surly and irritable initially, but ultimately began to cry. Eventually he spoke about his past.

His father lost his job when Michael was 9 and was unable to support Michael, his mother, and his three siblings. In desperation, Michael's father began to sell drugs. Michael's mother began to use the drugs and soon was unable to care for her four children. They were placed in foster care.

Michael reported living in five foster homes; lack of continuity undermined his educational success. He had seen none of his siblings for some time and knew nothing of their whereabouts or of his parents' well-being. He revealed that he had suffered crying spells for over a year (Bell, 1997).

The supply of African American clinicians is important. Studies of medical care reveal that African American physicians are five times more likely than White physicians to treat African American patients (Komaromy et al., 1996; Moy & Bartman, 1995) and that African American patients rate their physicians' styles of interaction as more participatory when they see African American physicians (Cooper-Patrick et al., 1999).

Mental Health United States reported that, among clinically trained mental health professionals, only 2 % of psychiatrists, 2% of psychologists, and 4% of social workers, identified as African American (Holzer et al., 1998). African Americans who seek help and would prefer an African American provider, will have difficulty finding such one in these prominent mental health specialties.

The availability of mental health services also depends on where one lives. As discussed earlier, a relatively high proportion of African Americans live in the rural South. Evidence indicates that mental health professionals are concentrated in urban areas and are less likely to be found in the most rural counties of the United States (Holzer et al., 1998). Furthermore, African Americans living in urban areas are often concentrated in poor communities; urban practitioners who do not accept Medicaid or offer services to high-need clientele are not available to them.

Accessibility of Mental Health Services

Lack of health insurance is a barrier to mental health care. Nearly one-fourth of African Americans are uninsured (Brown et al., 2000), a percentage 1.5 times greater than the White rate. In the United States, health insurance is typically provided as an employment benefit. Because African Americans are more often employed in marginal jobs, the rate of employer-based coverage among employed African Americans is substantially lower than the rate among employed whites (53% versus 73%; Hall et al., 1999).

Although insurance coverage is one of the most important determinants for deciding to seek treatment among both African Americans and Whites, it is clear that insurance alone—at least when provided by private sector plans, fails to eliminate disparities in access between African Americans and Whites (Scheffler & Miller, 1989; Snowden & Thomas, 2000). Provision of insurance benefits with more generous mental health coverage does not increase treatment seeking as much among African Americans as among whites (Padgett et al., 1995). Overcoming financial barriers is an important step in eliminating disparities in care; however, according to evidence currently available, it is not in itself sufficient.

Medicaid, a major public health insurance program subsidizing treatment for the poor, covers nearly 21% of African Americans. Medicaid payments are among the principal sources of financing for the services of safety net providers on which many African Americans depend. Medicaid-funded providers have been more successful than others in reducing disparities in access to mental health treatment (Snowden & Thomas, 2000).

African American attitudes toward mental illness are another barrier to seeking mental health care. Mental illness retains considerable stigma, and seeking treatment is not always encouraged. One study found that the proportion of African Americans who feared mental health treatment was 2.5 times greater than the proportion of Caucasians (Sussman et al., 1987).

Another study of parents of children meeting criteria for AD/HD discovered that African American parents were less likely than Caucasian parents to describe their child's difficulties using specific medical labels and more likely to expect a shorter term course (Bussing et al., 1998). Yet another study indicated that older African Americans were less knowledgeable about depression than elderly Caucasians (Zylstra & Steitz, 1999).

Practitioners and administrators have sometimes failed to take into account African American preferences in formats and styles of receiving assistance. African Americans are affected especially by the amount of time spent with their providers, by a sense of trust, and by whether the provider is an African American (Keith, 2000). Among focus group participants, African Americans were more likely than Caucasians to describe stigma and spirituality as affecting their willingness to seek help (Cooper-Patrick et al., 1997).

Children and Youth

African American and Caucasian American children receive outpatient mental health treatment at differing rates. Using the National Medical

Expenditure Survey, a large, community survey, Cunningham and Freiman (1996) discovered that African American children were less likely than Caucasian children to have made a mental health outpatient visit. The difference could not be attributed to underlying socioeconomic, family-related, or regional differences between the groups. Among children who received outpatient mental health treatment, African Americans and Caucasians had similar rates of receiving care from a mental health specialist.

A handful of smaller studies support this finding. One of them considered mental health care provided by specialists, by physicians and nurses, and in the schools (Zahner & Daskalakis, 1997). African American children and youth were less likely than Caucasians to receive treatment, and their underrepresentation varied little, no matter which source of treatment was used. Other school-based studies have reported similar findings Cuffe et al., 1995; Costello et al., 1997.

Perhaps because of lack of health insurance, few African American children are in psychiatric inpatient care (Chabra et al., 1999), but there are many in residential treatment centers (RTCs) for emotionally disturbed youth (Firestone, 1990). RTCs provide residential psychiatric treatment similar to that available in hospitals, but they are more likely to be funded from public sources.

In many cases, it is not parents, but child welfare authorities who initiate treatment for African American children. The child welfare system is a principal gate-keeper for African American mental health care Halfon et al., 1992; Takayama et al., 1994. For this reason, several studies focusing on metropolitan areas have found an overrepresentation of African American children and youth in public mental health services (Bui & Takeuchi, 1992; McCabe et al., 1999). However, access via the child welfare system often does not result in beneficial treatment.

Older Adults

Little evidence is available documenting the use of mental health services by older Black adults. However, one study found that these adults, like their younger counterparts, often do not obtain care (Black et al., 1997). In fact, this study reported that 58% of older African American adults with mental disorders were not receiving care. Another study indicated that older Blacks in long-term care were less likely to use available community services than were older Whites in long-term care (Mui & Burnette, 1994).

Complementary Therapies

African Americans are thought to make extensive use of alternative treatments for health and mental health problems. This preference is deemed to reflect African American cultural traditions developed partly when African Americans were systematically excluded from mainstream health care institutions (Smith Fahie, 1998).

Joan, a 50-year-old African American woman, was hospitalized following a suicide attempt. She cried and was nearly mute, reporting only her inability to sleep and that she heard voices commanding her to kill herself. Her medical records indicated a previous admission for psychotic depression. Joan recovered after she took antidepressant medication.

In response to questioning, Joan indicated that she had been successfully treated before, but that she had discontinued psychiatric medication after responding to a letter from an itinerant minister. He had administered holy oil in exchange for payment and informed her to stop taking medication because she had been cured. After relating this story, Joan was supported in her religious belief and in seeking spiritual uplift from one of many legitimate religious institutions in her community. She was warned, however, against opportunists and charlatans (Bell, 1997).

However, there is scant empirical data on the use of complementary therapies among African Americans suffering from mental health or other health problems (Koss-Chioino, 2000). Preliminary community and clinic-based studies have found that complementary therapies are used to treat anxiety and depression (Elder et al., 1997; Davidson et al., 1998) and to treat health problems that occur in conjunction with mental health problems (Druss & Rosenheck, 2000). One nationally representative survey indicated that African Americans held more favorable views toward use of home remedies than did Whites (Snowden et al., 1997).

Diagnostic Issues

Appropriate care depends on accurate diagnosis. Carefully gathered evidence indicates that African Americans are diagnosed accurately less often than White Americans when suffering from depression and seen in primary care (Borowsky et al., 2000), or for psychiatric evaluation in an emergency room (Strakowski et al., 1997).

For many years, clinicians and researchers observed a pattern whereby African Americans in treatment presented higher than expected rates of diagnosed schizophrenia and lower rates of diagnosed affective disorders (Neighbors et al.,1989). When structured procedures were used for assessment, or when retrospective assessments were made via chart review, the disparities between African Americans and Whites failed to emerge (Baker & Bell, 1999).

One explanation for the findings is clinician bias: Clinicians are predisposed to judge African Americans as schizophrenic, but not as suffering from an affective disorder. One careful study of psychiatric inpatients found that African Americans had higher rates of both clinical and research-based diagnoses of schizophrenia (Trierweiler et al., 2000). The clinicians in the study were well trained and included both African Americans and White Americans. However, it was found that they applied different decision rules to African American and White patients in judging the presence of schizophrenia. The role of clinician bias in accounting for this complex problem has not yet been ascertained.

Evidence-Based Treatments

In a nationally representative telephone and mail survey conducted in 1996, African Americans were found to be less likely than White Americans to receive appropriate care for depression or anxiety. Appropriate care was defined as care that adheres to official guidelines based on evidence from clinical trials. (Wang et al., 2000). Similar findings emerged in another large study that examined a representative national sample (Young et al., 2001). One large study of antidepressant medication use included all Medicaid recipients who had a diagnosis of depression at some time between 1989 and 1994 (Melfi et al., 2000). This study found that African Americans were less likely than Whites to receive an antidepressant when their depression was first diagnosed (27% versus 44%). Of those who did receive antidepressant medications, African Americans were less likely to receive the newer selective serotonin reuptake inhibitor (SSRI) medications than were the White clients.

This is important because the SSRIs have fewer troubling side effects than the older antidepressants; therefore, they tend to be more easily tolerated, and patients are less likely to discontinue taking them. Failure to treat with SSRI medications may be widespread and might help to explain African American overrepresentation in inpatient facilities and emergency rooms. Also, in a large study of older community residents followed from 1986 through 1996, Whites in 1986 were nearly twice as likely, and in 1996, almost

4 times more likely, to use an antidepressant than were African Americans (Blazer et al., 2000).

Best Practices

Biological similarities between African Americans and Caucasians are such that effective medications are suitable for treating mental illness in both groups. At the same time, recent evidence suggests that African Americans and Caucasian sometimes have different dosage needs. For example, a greater percentage of African Americans than Caucasian metabolize some antidepressants and antipsychotic medications slowly and might be more sensitive than their Caucasian counterparts (Ziegler & Biggs, 1977; Rudorfer & Robins, 1982; Bradford et al., 1998).

This higher sensitivity is manifested in a faster and higher rate of response overall (et al., 1969; Henry et al., 1971; Raskin & Crook, 1975; Ziegler & Biggs, 1977) and more severe side effects, including delirium (Livingston et al., 1983), when treated with doses commonly used for Whites. However, clinicians in psychiatric emergency services prescribe both more and higher doses of oral and injectable antipsychotic medications to African Americans than to Caucasians (Segel et al., 1996), as do other clinicians working in inpatient services (Chung et al., 1995). Other studies suggest that African Americans are also likely to receive higher overall doses of neuroleptics than Caucasian (Marcolin, 1991; Segel et al., 1996; Walkup et al., 2000).

The combination of slow metabolism and overmedication of antipsychotic drugs in African Americans can yield extra-pyramidal side effects, including stiffness, jitters, and muscle cramps (Lin et al., 1997), as well as increased risk of long-term severe side effects such as tardive dyskinesia, marked by abnormal muscular movements and gestures. Tardive dyskinesia has been shown in several studies to be significantly more prevalent among African Americans than among Whites (Morgenstern & Glazer, 1993; Glazer et al., 1994; Eastham & Jeste, 1996; Jeste et al., 1996).

African Americans have made great strides in education, income, and other indicators of social well-being. Their improvement in social standing is marked, attesting to the resilience and adaptive traditions of African American communities in the face of slavery, racism, and discrimination. Contributions have come from diverse African American communities, including immigrants from Africa, the Caribbean, and elsewhere. Nevertheless, significant problems remain.

Facing Unique Challenges

African Americans living in the community appear to have overall rates of distress symptoms and mental illness similar to those of Whites, although some exceptions may exist. One major epidemiological study found that the rates of disorder for Whites and Blacks were similar after controlling for differences in income, education, and marital status. A later, population-based study found similar rates before accounting for such socioeconomic variables. Furthermore, the distribution of disorders may be different between groups, with African Americans having higher rates of some disorders and lower rates of others.

The mental health of African Americans cannot be evaluated without considering the many African Americans found in high-need populations whose members have high levels of mental illness and are significantly in need of treatment. Proportionally, 3.5 times as many African Americans as Caucasian are homeless. None of them are included in community surveys. Other inaccessible populations also compound the problem of making accurate measurements and providing effective services.

The mental health problems of persons in high-need populations are especially likely to occur jointly with substance abuse problems, as well as with HIV infection or AIDS (Lewin & Altman, 2000). Detection, treatment, and rehabilitation become particularly challenging in the presence of multiple and significant impediments to well-being.

African Americans who are distressed or have a mental illness may present their symptoms according to certain idioms of distress. African American symptom presentation can differ from what most clinicians are trained to expect and may lead to diagnostic and treatment planning problems. The impact of culture on idioms of distress deserves more attention from researchers.

African Americans may be more likely than White Americans to use alternative therapies, although differences have not yet been firmly established. When complementary therapies are used, their use may not be communicated to clinicians. A lack of provider knowledge of their use may interfere with delivery of appropriate treatment.

Disparities in access to mental health services are partly attributable to financial barriers. Many of the working poor, among whom African Americans are overrepresented, do not qualify for public coverage and work in jobs that do not provide private coverage. Better access to private insurance is an important step but is not in itself sufficient. African American reliance on public financing suggests that provisions of the Medicaid program are also important. Publicly-financed safety net providers are a critical resource in the provision of care to African American communities.

Disparities in access also come about for reasons other than financial ones. Few mental health specialists are available for those African Americans who prefer an African American provider. Furthermore, African Americans are overrepresented in areas where few providers choose to practice. They may not trust or feel welcomed by the providers who are available. Feelings of mistrust and stigma or perceptions of racism or discrimination may keep them away.

African Americans with mental health needs are unlikely to receive treatment, even less likely than the under-treated mainstream population. If treated, they are likely to have sought help from primary care providers. African Americans frequently lack a usual source of health care as a focal point for treatment. Those who also receive specialty care tend to leave treatment prematurely. Mental health care occurs relatively frequently in emergency rooms and psychiatric hospitals. These settings and patterns of treatment undermine delivery of high-quality mental health care.

African Americans are more likely to be incorrectly diagnosed than Whites. They are more likely to be diagnosed as suffering from schizophrenia and less likely to be diagnosed as suffering from an affective disorder. The pattern is long-standing but cannot yet be fully explained.

Whether African Americans and Whites benefit from mental health treatment in equal measure is still under investigation. The limited information available suggests African Americans respond favorably for the most part, but few clinical trials have evaluated the response of African Americans to evidence-based treatments. Little research has examined the impact on African Americans of care delivered under usual conditions of community practice. More remains to be learned about when and how treatment must be modified to take into account African American needs and preferences.

Adaptive traditions have sustained African Americans through long periods of hardship imposed by the larger society. Their resilience is an important resource from which much can be learned. African American communities must be engaged, their traditions supported and built upon, and their trust gained in attempts to reduce mental illness and increase mental health. Mutual benefit will accrue to African Americans and to the society at large from a concerted effort to address the mental health needs of African Americans.

African Americans frequently lack a usual source of health care as a focal point for treatment. Those who also receive specialty care tend to leave treatment prematurely. Mental health care occurs relatively frequently in emergency rooms and psychiatric hospitals. These settings and patterns of treatment undermine delivery of high-quality mental health care.

People of color, particularly African Americans, feel the stigma more keenly. In a race-conscious society, some don't want to be perceived as having yet another deficit.
Bebe Moore Campbell, author

Chapter 5
Mistrust

Numerous African Americans may not consider mental health treatment as it is not something that is straightforwardly encouraged in everyday life (McGoldrick, Giordano and GarciaPreto, 2005). The 2012 National Healthcare Disparities Report announced that between the long periods of 2008-2010, African American teenagers and adults were less inclined to get treatment than White adults and teenagers (U.S Department of Health and Human Services, 2013). National epidemiologic appraisals show that while variations exist for certain issues, the predominance of genuine psychological maladjustment in African Americans is generally identical to that of Whites (Neighbors, Musick and Williams, 1998; Turner, Lloyd and Taylor, 2006).

Shockingly, little opportunity has been afforded to African Americans to verbalize their stories and likely complaints about the emotional challenges they face. There are likewise not very many studies that permit African Americans a chance to express smudges of disgrace and generalizations in a private one-on-one setting with an White medical professionals. Exploration has recognized a few purposes behind the absence of African American customers in treatment, for example, question of White emotional wellness advisors, bigotry, and the African American impression of treatment (Nickerson, Helms and Terrell, 1994; Williams and Williams-Morris, 2000; Thompson, Bazile and Akbar, 2004).

While the mental health field has found a way to make therapy more appealing to African Americans, there is still a great deal of research and work needed to find approaches to encourage African Americans to enter treatment. A 1996 overview on clinical depression by Mental Health America (MHA) recognized a few hindrances to the treatment of African Americans.

These responses include: a disavowal of an emotional well-being issues, humiliation/disgrace, didn't need assistance, couldn't bear the cost of treatment or didn't have protection, were excessively apprehensive, did not think enough about treatment, or felt too miserable to even think about seeking treatment (Mental Health America, 1996).

Every one of these explanations can be addressed if stigmas and stereotypes surrounding therapy are dispelled. The African American culture is very collective in its thinking. Coon and Kemmelmeier (2001) found that on average African Americans scored higher than European Americans on collectivism. In this study, collectivism is defined as people who identify themselves as embedded in groups and relationships. The collective thinking that surrounds the African American community contributes to the stereotype that all African Americans must be similar, and to stray from that mold casts someone as an outsider or an anomaly. It is essential to understand the degree to which culture impacts the decision for African Americans to attend therapy.

It is fundamental to comprehend how much culture impacts the choice for African Americans to go to treatment. Many of my Black clients have expressed belief that racism is a core element in the American macroculture. Therefore, they expect that institutions perceived as being created and controlled by the "white establishment" will not treat them fairly. Provider discrimination, including bias and stereotyping on the part of providers, is another source of disparities (Smedley et al., 2002). However, no research that we know of to date makes the empirical link between the stereotypic belief or bias and actual clinical discrimination.

One recent study comes close by using innovative methods to measure stereotypes and links to physician recommendations based on case vignettes randomized by race, but the link to actual practice remains speculative. The stigma of mental health isn't new to the Black community. Dr. Martin Luther King Jr. reportedly had severe depression during periods of his life and refused psychiatric treatment, even when urged to seek care by his staff. Unfortunately, that scenario continues to be common today with African Americans who refuse mental health care because of stigma. Understanding minority help-seeking behaviors for mental health services is a complex topic. There are several individual and systematic factors at play.

Community - Stigma and Discrimination

Mental health and treatment is still a primarily Western and European construct. Mental Health America conducted a survey and found that 63% of African Americans believe that depression is a "personal weakness." Many cultures operate from stoicism and emotional restriction. Because of this, individuals may be hesitant to seek mental health treatment in fear of shame and disgrace from their family, friends, and community.

Distinctive Challenges

Minority populations are less likely to know and understand mental disorders, symptoms, and treatment in the United States. For many minority populations, there is significant distrust and fear in the system. There are fears that mental health professionals may not understand or pathologize unique challenges the minority client may experience, such as discrimination, acculturation issues, and lack of access to resources. For example, African-Americans are more likely to be misdiagnosed with schizophrenia. It is critical that mental health professionals understand clients' context and culture to provide quality care.

Systemic Barriers

Many minority populations have less access to resources, such as insurance, transportation, and culturally-sensitive treatment. Individuals who have lower forms of insurance tend to receive less quality of care. There is also less availability and awareness of resources among minority communities. Therefore, minority clients are less likely to utilize resources, even if there are available.

In 2018, 8.7% of African American adults received mental health services compared with 18.6% of non-Hispanic White adults.

6.2% of African American adults received prescription medication for mental health services compared with 15.3% of non-Hispanic white adults.

In 2018, 3.8% of African American adults reported serious psychological distress.

Implicit Bias

Bear in mind, in spite of its potential influence on quality of care, there is sparse research on the way physicians' perceptions of and beliefs about patients are affected by patient race or socioeconomic status. Provider attitudes and behavior are a target area for researchers and practitioners attempting to understand and eradicate inequitable health care (Smedley et al., 2003). Although overt discriminatory behavior in the United States may have declined in recent decades, covert discrimination and institutional bias are sustained by subtle, implicit attitudes that may influence provider behavior and treatment choices.

As a result, patients of color may be kept waiting longer for assessment or treatment than their White counterparts, or providers may spend more time with White patients than with patients of color. In addition, providers may vary in the extent to which they collaborate with patients in systematic though non-deliberate ways, in considering treatment options based on patients' characteristics.

Subtle biases may be expressed in several ways:
- Approaching patients with a dominant and condescending tone that decreases the likelihood that patients will feel heard and valued by their providers,
- Failing to provide interpreters when needed,
- Doing more, or less, thorough diagnostic work,
- Recommending different treatment options for patients based on assumptions about their treatment adherence capabilities, and
- Granting special privileges, such as after hour family visits to some while limiting visitation for other families.

Variation in provider behaviors may be driven in part or in full by positive and negative attitudes that providers hold toward various racial and ethnic groups. Negative attitudes toward certain social groups or personal characteristics often exist at the margins of awareness and are not easily accessible to individuals. Social psychology scholars have conceptualized prejudicial attitudes or bias as implicit and explicit (Ranganath et al., 2007).

Explicit attitudes are thoughts and feelings that people deliberately think about and can make conscious reports about. On the other hand, implicit attitudes often exist outside of conscious awareness, and thus are difficult to consciously acknowledge and control. These attitudes are often automatically activated and can influence human behavior without conscious volition. Racial/ethnic bias in attitudes (such as feeling that White people are nicer than Black people), whether conscious or not, can lead to prejudicial behavior. For example, a White provider may take more time with White patients than Black patients and therefore learn more about the White patients' needs and concerns.

Within the general population, significant research exists about implicit racial/ethnic bias. For example, White Americans tend to associate negative valence in general, and certain feelings such as fear and distrust, with Black Americans (Burgess et al., 2004). Such group notions are automatically activated and applied most often when people are busy, distracted, tired, and under pressure (Yzerbyt et al., 1998).

The cognitive effort to assess and process a person's individual characteristics appears to be greater than that required to quickly categorize a person into a particular group with particular characteristics (Burgess et al., 2004). Such short cuts in thinking may be useful in certain situations, but when providers are seeking to establish genuine working relationships with their patients and deliver equitable health care, fast thinking or quick categorization may get in the way.

For example, during a diagnostic examination with a Black adolescent, a provider may automatically presume that they are sexually active rather than asking open-ended questions about sexual activity and listening carefully to the responses. Some White health care providers maintain problematic explicit ideas about their Black American patients, viewing them as less intelligent, less able to adhere to treatment regimens, and more likely to engage in risky health behaviors than their White counterparts (van Ryn et al., 2000).

Hispanic/Latino/Latina patients too were viewed as unlikely to accept responsibility for their own care and more likely to be noncompliant with treatment recommendations (Mayo et al., 2007). Yet, even if explicit attitudes are modified, implicit bias among providers toward people of color is likely to remain and influence care in ways that perpetuate disparity and inequity. Thus, even if explicit attitudes demonstrate a desire to provide equitable care, health care providers may unintentionally interact with patients of color less effectively than with White patients, which may contribute to health disparities (Blair et al., 2007).

Many of my Black clients have expressed belief that racism is a core element in the American macroculture. Therefore, they expect that institutions perceived as being created and controlled by the "white establishment" will not treat them fairly. Provider discrimination, including bias and stereotyping on the part of providers, is another source of disparities.
Dr. Pamela Robinson, Author

Every great dream begins with a dreamer. Always remember, you have within you the strength, the patience, and the passion to reach for the stars to change the world.
Harriet Tubman, Underground Railroad Conductor

Chapter 6
The H.O.P.E. Culturally-Centered Model

The Spiritual Assessment

More than 80% of Americans perceive religion as important. Issues of belief can affect the health care encounter, and patients may wish to discuss spirituality with their physician. Many physicians report barriers to broaching the subject of spirituality. They are concerned that during sessions there may be a lack of time and experience to deal with spirituality, difficulty identifying patients who want to discuss spirituality, and the belief that addressing spiritual concerns is not a physician's responsibility.

Spiritual assessment tools such as the FICA, the HOPE questions, and the Open Invite, provide efficient means of eliciting patients' thoughts on this topic. The spiritual assessment allows physicians to support patients by stressing empathetic listening, documenting spiritual preferences for future visits, incorporating the precepts of patients' faith traditions into treatment plans, and encouraging patients to use the resources of their spiritual traditions and communities for overall wellness. Conducting the spiritual assessment also may help strengthen the physician-patient relationship and offer physicians opportunities for personal renewal, resiliency, and growth (Saguil et al., 2012).

Definitions

The *Merriam-Webster Dictionary* defines Spiritual as "of, relating to, consisting of, or affecting the spirit" or, alternatively, "concerned with religious values."

Religion is defined as "a personal set or institutionalized system of religious attitudes, beliefs, and practices."

Although persons who are religious may consider themselves spiritual, there are many who consider themselves spiritual but not religious. Because family physicians care for patients of all affiliations, creeds, and beliefs, I am using the term *spirituality* because of its greater inclusivity. Spiritual assessment is the process by which health care providers can identify a patient's spiritual needs pertaining to their mental health care.

Compass of Spiritual Beliefs

Mental Health has even more of an impact when it comes to communities that once were legally prohibited from seeking mental and emotional health support. And when they did seek such support, it often led to extreme punitive results. As a result, most people of color turned to the Black church to help them spiritually focus on addressing issues of depression, suicide, trauma, grief, etc., which in most cases has not proven to be sufficient.

Although the spiritual component is critical, it is equally critical to acknowledge that an individual may need to seek assistance from mental health professionals, primary care physicians, and counselors to be whole mentally, spiritually, physically, and emotionally (Robinson 2017). The perceived importance of spirituality by patients and mental health professionals, primary care physicians, and counselors is borne out by secular opinion polls, medical literature, hospital regulations, and clinical practice guidelines (Robinson 2017).

According to The Pew Forum African Americans reported the greatest degree of religious belief among all racial, ethnic groups across the United States (Pew Research Center 2015). Specifically, 97% of all African Americans reported belief in God, which 83% reporting belief in God *absolutely*, and 75% of African Americans reported religion was very important in their lives, compared with 53% of people in the general population.

This data, along with African Americans' reliance on extended family members and clergy when faced with psychiatric problems, suggest that there is a great need for collaboration between clergy, mental health professionals, primary care physicians, and counselors.

Recognizing a patient's needs is one of the most important steps to providing care. A Spiritual Assessment can be routinely administered during triage. After spiritual needs have been identified, the physician may incorporate the results of the assessment into patient care. The most basic thing a physician can do is listen compassionately. Regardless of whether patients are devout in their spiritual traditions, their beliefs are important to them.

By listening, physicians signal their care for their patients and recognition of this dimension of their lives. Empathetic listening may be all the support a patient requires (Saguil et al., 2012).

Definition - Spiritual Assessment

According to the St. Elizabeth's Hospital in Washington, D.C., the Chaplain Program, assessment is the process by which health care providers can identify a patient's spiritual needs pertaining to their mental health care. The determination of spiritual needs and resources, evaluation of the impact of beliefs on healthcare outcomes and decisions, and discovery of barriers to using spiritual resources, are all outcomes of a thorough spiritual assessment.

The St. Elizabeth's Hospital in Washington, D.C., the Chaplain Program, headed by Clark Aist, conducted a "Spiritual Needs Assessment" on each inpatient, concluding with a treatment plan that identifies religious/ spiritual needs and problems, role of pastoral intervention, and religious/spiritual activities recommended.

Below are assessment instruments that were developed by St. Elizabeth's Hospital in Washington, D.C., Chaplain Program.

HOPE Assessment

    H--Sources of hope, strength, comfort, meaning, peace, love and connection,
    O--The role of organized religion for the patient,
    P--Personal spirituality and practices, and
    E--effects on medical care and end-of-life decisions.

Spiritual Assessment Interview

A. Religious background and beliefs

1. What religion did your family practice when you were growing up?

2. How religious were your parents?

3. Do you practice a religion currently?

4. Do you believe in God or a higher power?

5. What have been important experiences and thoughts about God/Higher Power?

6. How would you describe God/Higher Power? Personal or impersonal? Loving or stern?

B. Spiritual meaning and values

1. Do you follow any spiritual path or practice (e.g., meditation, yoga, chanting)?

2. What significant spiritual experiences have you had (e.g., mystical experience, near-death experience, 12-step spirituality, drug-induced, dreams)?

C. Prayer experiences

1. Do you pray? When? In what way(s)?

2. How has prayer worked in your life?

3. Have your prayers been answered?

FICA

F- Faith and beliefs

1) What are your spiritual or religious beliefs?

2) Do you consider yourself spiritual or religious?

3) What things do you believe in that give meaning to your life?

I- Importance and Influence

1) Is it important in your life?

2) How does it affect how you view your problems?

The HOPE Culturally Centered Model (HCCM)

3) How have your religion/spirituality influenced your behavior and mood during this illness?

4) What role might your religion/spirituality play in resolving your problems?

C - Community

1) Are you part of a spiritual or religious community?

2) Is this supportive to you and how?

3) Is there a person or group of people you really love or who are really important to you?

A - Address

1) How would you like me to address these issues in your treatment?

The Emerging HOPE Culturally Centered Model (HCCM)

While there is limited evidence on the impact of culturally-sensitive health care models, culturally-responsive comprehensive diagnostic and treatment modalities have yielded positive outcomes in reducing depressive symptoms among ethnically and culturally diverse communities (Warren, 1994; Beauboeuf Lafontant, 2007). There is a need to establish comprehensive methods on how to deliver quality and effective mental health services within the context of demonstrating respect for the cultural orientation of the patient.

Health care professionals must be able to provide effective care for increasingly diverse communities; and the cultural diversity of the health workforce must reflect diversity in society. Lack of diversity and cross-cultural skills in professional practice may contribute to continued growth in health disparities in the United States. For example, as previously indicated, ethnic minorities are less likely to engage in health promotion and disease prevention activities (Wilcox, Bopp, Oberrecht, Kammermann, & McElmurray, 2003).

Therefore, central to the focus of a culturally centered model of comprehensive health care for ethnic minorities should include aims of promoting health equity and reducing health disparities (Tucker et al., 2011; Rust et al., 2006). Implementing health care models that appreciate and respect the wide array of cultural backgrounds is an important strategy in addressing these disparities. Culturally-centered integrated care models must be patient centered, value cultural humility among providers, and be implemented in physical environments that respect and appreciate patient diversity and represented cultures (Tucker et al., 2011). These factors may facilitate a greater degree of trust among patients, health care providers, and clinic staff.

Culturally-centered health care also conceptualizes the patient–provider relationship as a partnership that emerges from patient centeredness and it is empowerment oriented (Tucker et al., 2007).What is missing from many of the comprehensive models is a cultural underpinning that may yield to better engagement of patients, their adherence to prescribed treatments, and improvement of their general wellbeing and quality of life.

Thus, I developed Emerging HOPE Culturally Centered Model (HCCM). The HCCM standard is a coordinated care service delivery model that includes behavioral health and primary care, and is indicative of important benefits to pursuing integration and collaboration. HCCM emphasizes the importance of understanding and respecting the patient's values and cultural background. The HCCM can guide professionals in an integrated behavioral health care setting to provide culturally competent mental health care.

The model examines how a patient interprets and express his or her spirituality and the role it plays in his or her life. The information gained can be beneficial with diagnosis and treatment. Moreover, HCCM is particularly significant for African American patients who value principles such of harmony, balance, interconnectedness, cultural awareness, and authenticity (Phillips, 1990).

A Bidirectional Approach

HCCM was based on the framework for the clinical integration of faith-based and behavioral health services. It expresses the need for a bidirectional approach, addressing the need for faith-based services in behavioral health settings, as well as the need for behavioral health services in primary care settings. HCCM is a model for how effective partnerships can be created between primary care, behavioral health, and faith-based organizations.

Through my research, I have found that assessing and integrating patient spirituality into the health care encounter can build trust and rapport, broadening the physician-patient relationship and also increasing its

The HOPE Culturally Centered Model (HCCM)

effectiveness. In turn, this could result in a vast number of useful outcomes, including increased loyalty to physician-recommended lifestyle changes, or compliance with therapeutic recommendations. Additionally, the assessment may help patients recognize spiritual or emotional challenges that are affecting their physical and mental health. Addressing spiritual issues may let them tap into an effective source of healing or coping.

Yet, great care must be forged to ensure patient self-reported information is not misconstrued. Without a careful and culturally-base spiritual assessment, those that express drawing strength from the use of spiritual warfare (i.e., laying on of hands as part of prayer for divine healing and the anointing of the sick, fasting and prayer, and quoting powerful warfare scriptures), may be misunderstood as expressing somatic delusions by health care professionals. Thereby, the patient may be susceptible to obtain a psychotic illness diagnosis that could result in substantial psychological duress that could lead to inappropriate treatment, deleterious treatment measures, and eventual premature termination of treatment by the patient.

Subsequently, a culturally relevant health care team that considers religious beliefs, culture, shows respect, and assesses and affirms the patient will be most effective when building rapport and partnership with the patient for treatment. Likewise, a culturally relevant environment must be forged so that the person is comfortable expressing their spiritual beliefs and their mental health concerns for a culturally-based, unbiased assessment.

Moreover, there may be some instances in which physician and patient faith traditions coincide. In these cases, if the patient requests, the physician may consider offering faith-specific support. This may include patient or physician-led prayer. Given the variety of spiritual practices followed in multicultural societies, it is best not to assume that a physician's spirituality mirrors that of his or her patients. Prayer should not be a goal of a spiritual assessment, and physicians should not attempt to get patients to agree with them on specific faith issues.

The HCCM encourage the provide to document the patient's spiritual perspective, background, stated impact on medical care, and openness to discussing the topic. This information can be useful to physicians when re-addressing the subject in the future or during times of crisis when sources of comfort and meaning become crucial. Hospital regulatory requirements for conducting a spiritual assessment can also be met by this documentation.

Moreover, as a culturally congruent model, HCCM recognizes core values and ways of being. For example, spirituality and religious practice as well as the role of the extended family are important sources of emotional, social, and material support for ethnic minorities in health care settings (Belgrave & Allison, 2010), and should be incorporated in comprehensive health care models developed for this population.

HCCM offers a conceptual framework for consideration of integrated care among African Americans, which may have applicability for other ethnic minorities. It proposes a culturally centered integrated care model that may be used by religious leaders, psychologists, psychiatrists, and family medicine providers in a faith based, behavioral health, and primary care setting to help promote better mental health among African Americans.

Another key feature of the HCCM is that implementing it within a practice setting requires not only individual level change but a change in practice culture. This paradigm shift covers mental and physical domains, such that the entire practice is transformed to embrace and adopt shared perspectives, expectations, and beliefs reflective of the African American culture. Moreover, because HCCM targets many of the challenges faced by African Americans in behavioral and health settings, it provides a practice infrastructure that is central to the proposed culturally centered integrated care model.

Overall, respect in the HCCM model implies that individuals have the right to receive respect according to their own personal perspective. Simple interventions, like asking the patient what will help them feel respected, is conducive to better professional–patient interaction. In turn, respect fosters trust. Assessing the patient's cultural history is often important and should be done for each patient, taking care not to make assumptions about individuals based on group membership. Moreover, an interest should be taken to ask simple questions such as: "Tell me about your family background," which can help practitioners learn more about the patient.

Subsequently, their cultural experience is affirmed. Likewise, sensitivity and self-awareness components of the HCCM compel mental health and medical professionals to be keen on specific perceptions within cultures. Being culturally sensitive and aware keeps mental health and medical professionals from breaking trust with the patient. Furthermore, understanding our cultural views and biases is important to be fully self-aware. Additionally, HCCM encourages the importance of humility. It is difficult for any individual to be completely culturally competent. Yet, this model compels the mental health and medical professionals to commit to learning from his or her patients and to make this a lifelong commitment.

Offering an apology for a cultural misstep gives the patient solace while providing a learning opportunity for the medical professional. Much mental health and medical professionals are in a unique role since they often encounter patients when they are at their most vulnerable. We believe that it is important for us to realize this and to provide comfort. A component to this is to offer acknowledgment of their cultural story, which strengthens the therapeutic bond in a way that promotes cultural sensitivity and facilitates the implementation of a mental health care delivery system that has the potential to remove many of the barriers that ethnically and culturally diverse populations experience in other health care settings.

After diabetes and hypertension, mental illness is the third most common reason patients seek treatment at a health care facility. The rates of mental health problems are significantly higher for patients with certain chronic conditions, such as diabetes, asthma, and heart conditions (USDHHS, 2012). The health care team, with the patient at the center, and an environment that enhances access, equals quality, and safety. The integration of services also contributes to a reduction in patients' reluctance to pursue mental health and behavioral health services, in addition to reduced language and cultural barriers.

The proposed HCCM model recommends for mental health practitioners who work with ethnically and culturally diverse clients/patients include establishing a strong collaborative partnership with behavioral health and primary care physicians. This will allow for enhanced bidirectional communication and information exchange about client/patient health and mental health issues. In addition, it will improve care coordination and the likelihood of identifying risk and protective factors that may contribute to treatment planning, adherence, and improved outcomes. It allows practitioners to assess cultural biases, stereotypes, and ethnocentric views that may impact the establishment of a rapport with clients seeking care.

Moreover, this will help further sensitize practitioners to psychosocial, sociocultural, and environmental issues that may contribute to symptom severity and related concerns, as well as promote a nonjudgmental position. They can use faith-based and culturally-sensitive assessment methods for screening and treatment of clients. This will include recognition of aspects of culturally-derived practices and norms of clients of African descent, and acknowledge the role of faith-based culturally-centered behavioral health care.

Although cultural competence is rarely fully actualized, it is helpful to consistently aspire toward increased learning and understanding about cultural differences among various ethnic groups. Overall, recognition of the value in promoting culturally-centered integrated care and implementation of strategies will help contribute to the reduction of mental health disparities and promote better health, mental health, and well-being.

HISTORY of EMERGING HOPE FAMILY STRENGTHENING PROGRAM

When her youngest daughter Carmela was 7 months old, Pamela and her husband divorced. Now a single parent, she was left to raise three small children on her own. She was a heartbroken 30-year-old left to live in the "projects" (a.k.a. Public Housing) left to rely on government assistance.

That first year was chaos. It did not help that there were no single-mom role models in her life, and her family lived miles away. Fortunately, she had a fantastic church family who helped. Maybe none of them knew exactly what she was going through, but they baby sat and showered her and the kids with love, which she appreciates to this day.

In the wake of this staggering life circumstance, she saw an opportunity to reframe the situation of being a single parent into a positive resource for her and other single parents who passed through similar treacherous waters she had been able to successfully navigate because of God's unconditional grace and mercy.

2002

In 2002, Pamela founded The Emerging HOPE Family Strengthening Program, LLC as a practical family fortifying program committed to provide ethnically-diverse marginalized individuals, single-parent households, and families with the tools, resources, and services to promote healthy individual and family functioning.

Emerging HOPE humbly started as an educational program that offered culturally-relevant parenting classes to under-resourced, marginalized single parent households. Moreover, utilizing her own life experience as a former single parent, Pamela wrote the multicultural-interactive curriculum for the parenting classes which taught how to strengthen family dynamics by managing finances, enhancing parental relations, and navigating community services.

Bread
for the
Journey
of Southwest
Michigan

Nurturing
neighborhood
philanthropy

Dear Pamela,
 Best wishes in your good work! It was a pleasure to meet you.
 Sincerely,
 Karen H-g

The healing of the world will only grow
in the sweet soil of relationships—relationships built
on love, faith and quiet kindness.
—Wayne Muller

History

Since its inception, Emerging HOPE participants have experienced an increase in self-esteem, learned budgeting skills, cultivated educational goals for their families, and regained custody of their children. The results:
- 25% of the participants enrolled in courses completed their GED's,
- 10% enrolled in community college,
- 30% of their preteen children and 50% of the parents enrolled as volunteers with the Kalamazoo Volunteer Center to serve in the community,
- 80% of participants' children received full camp scholarships to attend the West Michigan Glass Society, the Kalamazoo Nature Center, Sherman Lake YMCA, and Beech Point Christian Camp.

2003

With great enthusiasm and drive to offer additional services, in 2003, Emerging HOPE was awarded a generous grant from the local Kalamazoo Community Foundation (under the fiduciary agent of the Kalamazoo Dream Center) to support its family strengthening classes.

2007

In 2007, Emerging HOPE was awarded a second grant from Kalamazoo Community Foundation to facilitate one year of parenting classes that utilized her unique Emerging HOPE curriculum at Family & Children Services.

2008

In January 2008, Emerging HOPE looked for means to enlarge the capacity of the educational program to incorporate mental health counseling, life skill training, coaching, and mentoring. They were privileged to come in contact with *Bread for the Journey of Southwest Michigan*, a group of philanthropist who give microgrants to those with ideas to make community more healthy, just, and wonderful. This copious grant went to support the expansion of outreach services, website design, and the purchase of various office supplies. The greater part of Emerging HOPE funds was raised through private gifts, altruistic endowments, web giving, and fund-raising events.

That same year, Dr. Robinson founded Emerging HOPE Christian Counseling, an interdisciplinary private practice which provides cultur-

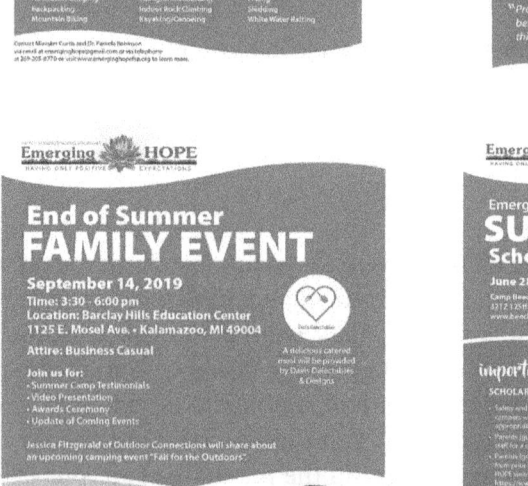

ally relevant mental health services and programming in partnership with clients. She soon was awarded a counseling contract with the Department of Health and Human Services (DHHS) Foster Care Program and worked as a contracted outreach therapist with several urban school districts.

Emerging HOPE has successfully partnered with culturally-diverse community agencies in Kalamazoo County such as: The Kalamazoo Dream Center, Kalamazoo Gospel Mission, New Focus National, Fox Ridge Apartments, National Alliance on Mental Illness, New Genesis Incorporated, Family & Children Services, Bread for the Journey, West Michigan Glass Society, Kalamazoo Nature Center, Sherman Lake YMCA, Integrated Behavior Health, Gryphon Place, Living Water Ministries, Beach Point Christian Camp, The Volunteer Center of Kalamazoo, Project Connect, City of Kalamazoo MLK Day of Caring, and Northside Ministerial Alliance Martin Luther King, Jr. Community Celebration.

2010

In 2010, Emerging HOPE warmly welcomed an innovative codirector, Pamela's husband, Curtis Robinson, Sr. As a natural leader and gifted public speaker, he served in many service-oriented capacities in the urban-community. As Certified Recovery Coach, Peer Support Specialist and Pastoral Counselor, he had far-reaching individual and professional involvement in the psychological wellbeing and recuperation of people struggling with mental health and addictions.

In like manner, Emerging HOPE has respectfully worked together with many summer-day programs and residential summer camps and over the past twelve years to provide fun-filled summer experiences for urban youth. The program is designed to provide urban youth with safe and supportive community enrichment skills through recreational outdoor activities. Likewise, the program aims to increase social emotional skills, resiliency skills, leadership skills and address mental and emotional concerns whereby empowering youth to live healthy, fully functioning lives.

For ten consecutive summers, Emerging HOPE hosted a one-day community-wide event entitled "Camp Day Out." The purpose of this free family-fun event was to inform urban families with youth (ages 5-18) of camping opportunities that were available to their children. The event consists of on-site camp registration, free summer camp scholarships, music, door prizes, face painting, and other fun activities. Parents and youth have the opportunity to meet camp directors from an array of camps to learn about their programs. Most importantly, many of the programs awarded generous summer camp

scholarships to participants who attended the events.

Emerging HOPE has hosted twelve annual Mental Health Forums at strategic locations in Kalamazoo County. Dr. Robinson designed a replicable culturally relevant mental health model; whereby, enhancing the cultural relevance of empirically supported mental health interventions referenced in her dissertation. The model was utilized as the first African American Mental Health Wellness event in Kalamazoo County to embrace the topic of Mental Health disparities in the Black community.

The purpose of the forum was to empower participants and to bring awareness to a social cause. More specifically, the aim of the forum also was to decrease mental health stigma and increase awareness of mental health recovery in the African American community. Subsequently, throughout their years of hosting the forum, they learned that people need a healing community, whereby they can receive support and unconditional love in several ways. Additionally, they learned that hurting people desired, most of all, to know that they were not alone, and that someone else was willing to hear their story and would accept them after they share it. People needed to know that their pain did not mean God had turned His back on them.

Notably, the Forum was established to foster dialogue among a broad range of stakeholders—pastors, faith-based institutions, practitioners, policymakers, community members, recipients of services, and others—and to provide ongoing opportunities to confront issues of mutual interest and concern. Likewise, the Forum provided a neutral venue for broad-ranging discussions that aided in coordination and cooperation between public, faith-based, service recipients, and private stakeholders in eradicating the stigma of mental illness.

Incidentally, having diligently walked in obedience to God's Word, the soil was cultivated and made fertile as they laid a strong foundation, and planted seeds for a culturally-relevant mental health replicable model in Kalamazoo County. Recognizing that there was yet an abundance of work to do in the area of mental health disparities in the African American community, the Robinsons made mental health disparities a paramount part of their ministry.

2015

In effort to further educate the community about mental health disparities in the African American community, in March 2015, the Robinson's were featured guest on Valarie Lego's *Live at Five*–WZZM 13 Grand Rapids, Michi-

The Color of HOPE

gan. The focus of the interview was "Understanding the Impact of Stigma on People with Mental Illness." Moreover, each year, the forums have expanded to include an array of professionals, religious leaders, and support services. The forum's professional capacity expanded to the degree that Emerging HOPE was privileged to begin offering participants Western Michigan University Continuing Education Credits (CEU) and Michigan State Continuing Education Clock Hours (SCECH) for attending. Therefore, allowing the conference to be marketed to professionals who wanted to attend to obtain CEUs and SCECH to maintain licensure.

2016

On April 8, 2016, Dr. and Rev. Robinson were featured guest on National Public Radio, NPR with host Earlene McMichael as they shared about mental health disparities in the African American community.

Emerging HOPE is a ministry committed to preaching the gospel, evangelizing, educating, equipping and empowering under-resourced individuals, single-parent households, and families. The ministry provides participants with resources, practical assistance, emotional encouragement and social networking to better their lives, and those of their children. The go-to resource of Kalamazoo helps promote mental health in diverse communities, cultural perspectives on mental health, knowledge, hope, and healing to individuals, families, and communities touched by mental illness.

2019

In 2019, the Robinsons changed its tax-exempt status from LLC to a Nonprofit Corporation 501(c)(3). This change was made to fully reflect its mission of preaching the gospel, providing professional, effective leadership, and advocacy services to ethnically diverse individuals and families.

Likewise, the ministry expanded and added:
Men of HOPE Support Group • Empowering Worship Services
Bible Study • Culturally Relevant Counseling Services
Pastoral Counseling • Outreach Programs for Urban Youth
Brown Bag Support Group for therapist, clergy, Human Service professionals, and urban youth program leaders • Holiday Gift Baskets
Educational Workshops • Self Determination Living Consultation Services (Adults with Intellectual Disabilities)

The Color of HOPE

History

Our Guiding Principles are as follows:

- Emerging HOPE empowers socially and under-resourced parenting households towards self-sufficiency, while adding value to families.

- Emerging HOPE engages under-resourced individuals and families in meaningful activities to nurture leadership and influence in the community.

- Emerging HOPE strengthens under-resourced individuals and families through spiritual enrichment activities.

- Emerging HOPE empowers children, adolescents, and adults to live healthy, fully functioning lives.

- Emerging HOPE promotes the well-being of the individual, family, and community through programs, services, and information.

- Emerging HOPE utilizes strategies to help promote mental health in diverse communities.

- Emerging HOPE offers resources which are helpful in addressing and reducing minority mental health disparities.

- Emerging HOPE's interpersonal skills are our best quality. They are comfortable in presenting a positive public image interacting with potential donors and communicating with various levels of stakeholder.

- Emerging HOPE takes great pride in running a successful organization and in developing relationships.

- Emerging HOPE is committed to helping people live healthy lives.

Dr. Pamela and Rev. Robinson pride themselves on providing culturally relevant services in partnership with their participants. They have discovered the numerous advantages of serving together that go beyond bonding, contentment, and peace. There is a sweet intimacy that comes with working together on a service project or giving together to those in need. They believe that embracing God's call to serve together has strengthened and has added closeness to their relationship. There are special moments and memories that naturally come when they do things together. As an earth-shaking, cutting-edge couple, they make it their mission to help one another realize all the potential God has created in each of them. The Robinsons take pride in the fact that God has teamed them up to serve as co-directors of Emerging HOPE. They passionately believe that God intends for them to enjoy both ministry and marriage. "There's no one like us, and we were tailored-made for each other," Rev. Robinson says.

Likewise, participating together in ministry opportunities—whether in their church, neighborhood, community, or the world—has helped them to grow in their faith as a couple. Working side-by-side to fulfill the Great Commission, in whatever capacity, has deepened their spiritual intimacy. They find that being the Lord's witnesses through serving, giving, encouraging, caring, and loving as Jesus loved, is rewarding beyond words. According to the Robinsons, in the end, it is not about them. It is about the poor, the needy, and those who need a touch from God. Through it all, they often hear people tell them what a blessing it to see them in ministry together.

The Robinsons have found that because God has created man and woman to complete each other, having the full counsel of the male and the female perspective when confronting ministry issues is invaluable. Likewise, the opportunity to have both a woman and a man present to deal with issues relevant to each gender is a great benefit to their ministry. The Robinsons passionately believe effective team ministry begins with a healthy marriage and family grounded in a whole and holy relationship to the Father through Jesus Christ and empowered by the Holy Spirit. As a dynamic team of two, the Lord has placed a heavy mandate in their hearts to reach out into the marketplace and into the kingdom like never.

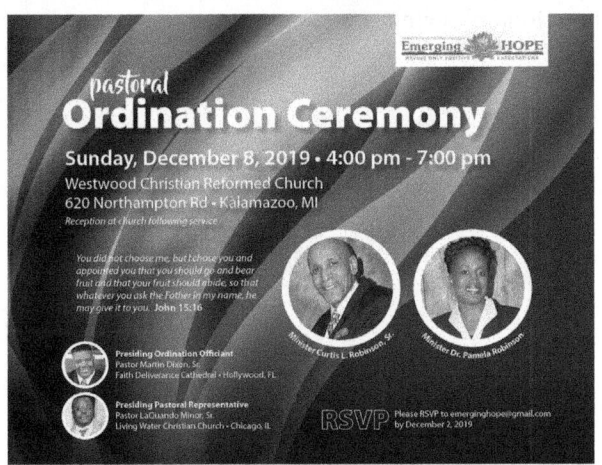

Appendices

Appendix A - Church Congregational Survey

Appendix B - Mental Health Awareness in the Church Survey

Appendix C - Sermon: "Call Them Here"

Appendix D - Faith Importance Community Address "Spiritual History Tool"

Appendix E - Hope Questions for Spiritual Assessment

Appendix F - The Open Invite Mnemonic

Appendix G - Doctoral of Ministry Dissertation Project

Appendix H - What is Psychotropic Medication Review Meeting?

Appendix I - Discussing Your Concerns with the Doctor: Worksheet

Appendix J - Psychotropic Medication Review: Questions About My Mood

Appendix K - Psychotropic Medication Review: Questions About My Sleep

Appendix L - Psychotropic Medication Review: Questions about My Appetite

Appendix M - Psychotropic Medication Review: Questions about Focus and Direction Following

Appendices

Appendix A

Church Congregational Survey

1. Which category below includes your age?
18-20
21-29
30-39
40-49
50-59
60 or older

2. What is your gender?
Male
Female

3. What is your marital status? (Select one)
Single
Living with Partner
Married
Divorced
Separated
Widowed

4. What is your affiliation with the congregation?
Member
Visitor
Regular attendee (non-member)
Watchcare
Other_____

5. How long have you been associated with the congregation?
Less than 1 year
1-2 years
3-5 years
6-10 years
11-15 years
16-20 years
21 years or more
Founding Member

6. **How often do you attend worship services?**
Very Frequently
Frequently
Occasionally
Rarely
Very Rarely

7. **What might our congregation offer to minister to people with mental health challenges (special needs)?**
   Please rank the importance of the following.
   (Please fill in your rank order using numbers 1 through 6 with 1 being the most important):

_____ Special Needs Worship Service

_____ Train leaders, congregational members, and staff in disability etiquette so that they are comfortable in their relationships with visitors and members who have disabilities.

_____ Invite speakers from the community, show awareness films and videos to help raise disability awareness dispel myths and eliminate stereo types about disabilities, etc.

_____ Support Groups for depression, anxiety, etc. other mental health challenges.

_____ Resources for adults and children on inclusion of persons with disabilities, as well as worship materials in alternative formats.

Other: _____

BARRIERS

8. **What do you think may hinder a person from seeking treatment such as (medication, therapy, coaching, and counseling) for mental health challenges (special needs)?**

____ Lack of knowledge about mental health services
____ Fear/stress about the act of seeking help
____ Lack of health insurance or coverage that leaves a large amount owing
____ Confidentiality, other people might find out
____ Stigma

Appendices

____ Embarrassment and fear of what other may think
____ Poor self perception, believing that one's behavior, emotion and mental state are normal
____ Lack of faith in God's ability to heal
____ Other (please specify)

ATTITUDES

9. When a person with special needs sits by you in church, how do you feel? (Check 2 or 3 that apply most)

____ Happy
____ Fearful
____ Timid
____ Ignorant
____ Mixed feeling between wanting to reach out but scared
____ Don't know how to act
____ Don't know how to feel
____ Awkward
____ Loving
____ Tentative
____ Inadequate
____ Welcoming
____ I want to move
____ Other (please state)…

ACCESSIBILITY

10. How could we make our congregation more inclusive and welcoming for people with mental health challenges (special needs)?
Please rank the importance of the following.
(Please fill in your rank order using numbers 1 through 5 with 1 being the most important):

____ State, all are welcome and provide a phone number to provide any needed accommodations in all event announcements.

____ Personally invite children and adults with mental health challenges to participate in ministries, religious education programs and events. Arrange for accommodations.

____ When new members join; ask in a sensitive and dignified way if any accommodations would enhance their participation in the faith community.

_____ Provide large print versions of the bulletin and worship materials are available.

_____ Other _____

INVISIBLE DISABILITIES

11. Invisible disabilities that are not immediately apparent such as a physical and mobility impairment (i.e. blindness, low vision, amputation, etc.). Have you experienced an invisible disability within yourself, your friends, or within someone in your family? Check all that you believe are invisible disabilities.

_____ Traumatic Brain Injuries
_____ Depression
_____ Anxiety
_____ Self-harm
_____ Eating disorders
_____ Bipolar disorder
_____ PTSD
_____ Borderline personality disorder
_____ Schizophrenia
_____ Alcoholism
_____ Prescription drug addiction
_____ Learning Disabilities
_____ Mild Multiple Sclerosis
_____ Hard of Hearing
_____ Chemical Sensitivities
_____ Heart Disease
_____ Arthritis
_____ Chronic Fatigue
_____ Celiac Disease
_____ Prescription Drug Use
_____ Other

Appendices

Closure – Additional Considerations

12. Who, me? A person with special needs came up and hugged me today. What were my reactions?

____ Say something encouraging, i.e., "you have such a beautiful smile."

____ Give non-verbal signs of approval.

____ Warmly embrace them.

____ I don't know how I would respond, especially if they seemed to dominate my time and the conversation.

____ I would feel uncomfortable.

____ We have nothing in common.

____ Other

13. How can we better serve people with mental health challenges (special needs)?

_____
_____
_____
_____

Appendix B

Mental Health Awareness in the Church (Survey)

1. **In Mark 10:46-52, the healing of Blind Bartimaeus, what did Jesus really cure?**
   a. ____Blindness
   b. ____Poverty
   c. ____Stigma
   d. ____All of the above

2. **Please circle the biblical characters who lived with a disability.**
   a. ____Paul
   b. ____Jacob
   c. ____Mephibostheth
   d. ____Man at the Pool of Bethesda
   e. ____All of the above

3. **What is an invisible disability?**
   a. ____Anxiety
   b. ____Depression
   c. ____Schizophrenia
   d. ____All of the above

4. **How do invisible disabilities lead to people being treated as though they are invisible?**
   a. ____By being stigmatized
   b. ____By being excluded
   c. ____By being oppressed
   d. ____All of the above

5. **What did Blind Bartimaeus mean when he said, "Jesus have mercy on me?" Mark 10:46-52**
   a. ____He was stating a welcoming affirmation
   b. ____Crying out for help
   c. ____Was identifying Jesus as the King
   d. ____All of the above

Appendices

6. **How do we make people with mental illness invisible in the church?**
a. ____Ignore them
b. ____No support groups or programs offered for them
c. ____Never mention mental illness in sermons or teaching lessons
d. ____Provide ministry to them instead of with them

7. **Jesus ministered to people who were physically, emotionally, and mentally sick.**
a. ____True
b. ____False

8. **People who experience a physical, emotional, or mental health crisis quite naturally call the church before they call anyone else.**
a. ____True
b. ____False

9. _____ is a condition that impacts a person's thinking, feeling or mood and may affect his or her ability to related to others and function on a daily basis.

10. **Why do Christians sometimes keep it a secret that they have mental illness?**
a. ____Stigma
b. ____Embarrassment
c. ____Fear
d. Rejection
e. ____Maybe seen as having little faith

11. **In the Christian community mental illness has been one of the church's "dirty little secrets." Why?**
a. ____Because the topic is consider taboo
b. ____Often fraught with misconception
c. ____Religious cultural barriers
d. ____All of the above

12. **How long was the man (John 5:1-6) lying by the Pool of Bethesda?**
a. ____One Year
b. ____Eight Years
c. ____Thirty-eight years
d. ____Since Birth

13. **Why didn't someone help the man that was lying by the Pool of Bethesda?**
a. ____Too busy with their own problems
b. ____Uncertain what to do
c. ____Fear
d. ____Would take up too much of their time
e. ____Other_____

Appendix C

Mental Health Inclusion…Preaching it From the Pulpit

Sermon - "Call Them Here"
Writer: Anonymous

There is a stigma around cognitive disabilities in this culture because, in the eyes of many people, mental illness doesn't count as a "real" disease, like cancer or the flu. Under the weight of this social stigma, we who live with mental illness often become "invisible people" who suffer silently and alone from the effects of our conditions. We are treated as failures, ne'er-do-wells, and misfits in a society that measures the "worth" of a person based on his or her ability to produce and consume in a capitalist economy.

In today's sermon, we encounter the story of a person, Bartimaeus, who was similarly "invisible" to the people of his own place and time.

There are several things it is important to note about Bartimaeus as a person. First of all, his name. In Aramaic, it literally means "son of Timaeus," which is to say that he really doesn't have a name or unique identity of his own. Yet, there is more to Bartimaeus than meets the eye on the surface. He might be visually impaired, but we the readers quickly learn that his spiritual insight goes deeper than that of his neighbors. He sees Jesus more clearly than anyone.

As Jesus draws near, Bartimaeus begins to make quite a fuss, calling out to Jesus as the "Son of David."

What Bartimaeus says to his Messiah next is "have mercy on me!"

This sounds to us like a plea for forgiveness, but is actually more like a welcoming affirmation. Caesar used to enter the city of Rome in triumphant procession with the citizenry crying "Lord, have mercy!" around him on every side. It's kind of like an ancient version of "Hail to the Chief" or "God Save the Queen". Bartimaeus has something unique to teach his people: he knows who Jesus really is, but they don't want to hear it, so they yell at him to sit back down and be quiet.

Sadly, this story is way too familiar for many of our brothers and sisters who live with disabilities, visible or invisible, in the church. As human institutions, churches often act like the crowd around Bartimaeus: ignoring and objectifying disabled people, pushing them to the edges of church life and telling them not to make too much of a fuss, so that business-as-usual can continue uninterrupted on Sunday morning.

What these churches don't realize is that every person is made uniquely in the image of God, therefore each individual has something to teach the rest of us about God that cannot be learned from anyone else on earth. Those who lose the most when disabled people are ignored are not the disabled people themselves, but those who ignore them. So it was with the crowd around Bartimaeus, and so it is in too many churches today.

But the good news is that Jesus is not content to simply walk by while this happens. Jesus listens to the voice of the voiceless and ensures that the lessons they teach will not go unheard. Looking closely at his interaction with Bartimaeus, we can get an idea of how Christ is working with disabled members in the church today, through the power of the Holy Spirit.

Point 1: To begin with, the first important thing that Jesus does is nothing. He simply stops. The text says he "stood still." What this tells us is that Jesus is willing to be interrupted by this person. Sure, Jesus is busy. Sure, he has other important things to do (go to Jerusalem and save the world, for instance). But business-as-usual gets put on the back burner for Jesus when it comes to having a relational encounter with this person. Imagine the church doing that!

Imagine what Christianity in this world would look like if the leaders of the church were willing to put aside their overcrowded schedules and interrupt business-as-usual in order to listen to the pained cries of needy people.

Point 2: The second thing Jesus does is say, "Call him here." He rearranges his ministry so that the marginalized person sits at the center of the action and concern. And he doesn't do it alone, either. Jesus could have easily called Bartimaeus over himself, but he enlists the help of the whole community, instead. So then, it is the crowd that changes its tune and says to Bartimaeus, "Take heart; get up, he is calling you."

Again, imagine the church doing this today: becoming a community that speaks forth Christ's calling on the lives of the very people whom the world ignores!

Point 3: The next thing Jesus does is give a voice back to the voiceless. Instead of presuming to know what is best for this other person, Jesus asks, "What do you want me to do for you?" This is a very important detail because Jesus is relating to Bartimaeus as a real person, not just as an object or problem to be dealt with. And when the miracle is said and done, Jesus even gives the credit back to Bartimaeus himself: "your faith has made you well."

Imagine a church focusing its ministry like this: interrupting business-as-usual to forge real, authentic relationships with people whose voices have not yet been heard in the mainstream of society. Imagine the church becoming a community where people are treated like people. Imagine a church that reorients its entire ministry to put marginalized people at the center of its life and action. Imagine a church that doesn't just welcome people who live with mental illness, but empowers them to fulfill their calling in Christ. Can you imagine a church like that?

Closing:

The "good word" of God has the power to frame the universe & the world from the beginning.

The "good word" of God has the power to cause dry bones to jump up and live.

The "good word" of God has the power to feel like "fire" shut up in my bones.

The "good word" of God has the power to raise a dead man back to life.

Something not to say from the pulpit . . .

Don't minimize the severity of mental illness

Don't question the validity of specific diagnoses

Don't question the legitimacy of treatments dispensed by licensed professionals

Don't attribute all mental illness to sin or to a lack of faith

Don't assume that spiritual remedies alone will be the only way in which God chooses to heal persons with mental illness

When the leader of your church talks about mental illness from the pulpit or the stage during weekend worship services, they communicate to the body that people with mental illness are valued and grant permission for members and attendees to talk with others in the church about their experiences.

Appendices

Appendix D

FICA Spiritual History Tool

Category	Sample questions
Faith and belief:	Do you have spiritual beliefs that help you cope with stress? If the person responds "no," consider asking: what gives your life meaning?
Importance	Have your beliefs influenced how you take care of yourself in this illness?
Community	Are you part of a spiritual or religious community?
Address in care	How would you like me to address these issues in your health care?

Adapted with permission from The George Washington Institute for Spirituality and Health. FICA spiritual history tool http://www.gwumc.edu

Appendix E

Hope Questions for Spiritual Assessment

Category	Sample questions
H: sources of hope	What are your sources of hope, strength, comfort, and peace?
O: organized religion	Are you part of a religious or spiritual community? Does it help you?
P: personal spirituality	Do you have person spiritual beliefs? What aspects of your spirituality or spiritual practices do you and practice find most helpful?
E: effects on medical care	Does your current situation affect your ability to do the things that usually help and end of life issues you spirituality?

As a doctor, is there anything that I can do to help you access the resources that usually help you?

Are there any specific practices or restrictions I should know about in providing your medical care?

If the patient is dying: How do your beliefs affect the kind of medical care you would like me to provide over the next few days/weeks/months?

Adapted with permission from Anandarajah G, Hight E. Spirituality and medical practice: using the HOPE questions as a practical tool for spiritual assessment. American Family Physician. 2001;63(1):87

Appendix F

The Open Invite Mnemonic

Category	Sample questions
Open (i.e., open the door to conversation)	May I ask your faith background? Do you have a spiritual or faith preference? What helps you through hard times?
Invite (i.e., invite the patient to discuss spiritual needs)	Do you feel that your spiritual health is affecting your physical health?
	Does your spirituality impact the health decisions you make?
	Is there a way in which you would like for me to account for your spirituality in your health care?
	Is there a way in which I or another member of the medical team can provide you with support?
	Are there resources in your faith community that you would like for me to help mobilize on your behalf?

Adapted with permission from Anandarajah G, Hight E. Spirituality and medical practice: using the HOPE questions as a practical tool for spiritual assessment. American Family Physician. 2001;63(1):87

The Color of HOPE

Appendix G

DOCTORAL MINISTRY PROGRAM
APEX SCHOOL OF THEOLOGY
DURHAM, NORTH CAROLINA

DOCTORAL OF MINISTRY DISSERTATION PROJECT
You are cordially invited to participate in a series of three educational workshops that will contribute to the completion of Pamela Robinson's Doctoral Dissertation Project.

DISSERTATION TITLE
"Same Lake-Different Boat: An Examination of the Attitudes, Values, Beliefs, and Behaviors of an African-American Faith Community Toward Adults with Intellectual Disabilities, Developmental Disabilities, and/or Mental Health Concerns."

EDUCATIONAL WORKSHOPS
March 19, 2016; 10:00am – 12:00pm
Having Your Voices Heard: A Community Conversation
Facilitated by: Dr. Luchara Wallace, PhD, Assistant Professor, WMU Special Education Program, DMin. Committee Chair.

March 26, 2016; 10:00am – 12:00pm
Mental Health Awareness in the Church
Facilitated by: Reverend Bruce Vaandrager, B.S., MDiv., Director of Mission and Culture, Pastoral Services Department Hope Network.

April 2, 2016; 10:00am – 12:00pm
What Would Jesus Do? Redefining how congregations respond to individuals with intellectual disabilities, developmental disabilities and/or mental health conditions. Facilitated by: Minister Curtis Robinson, Minister Pamela Robinson, and Reverend Barrett Lee.

Disclaimer
Any interpretations or analysis contained in this doctoral dissertation project represents the understanding and the opinions of the facilitators, are based solely on the information provided by the doctoral candidate and does not represent Galilee Baptist Church, a legal position, businesses, agencies, or any other entity, nor does it substitute for professional counseling.

DISSERTATION COMMITTEE
Dr. Luchara Wallace, Committee Chair

Minister Curtis Robinson
Dr. Michael T. Scott, Sr.
Dr. Tamara Scott
Dr. Lafayette Maxwell
Dr. Terry Thomas
Dr. Gladys Long
Dr. Cornelius Battle
Mr. Jermaine Harris
Minister Dorla Coleman-Bonner
Ms. Janet Harris, DMin Peer Associate
Reverend Barrett Lee

DISSERTATION PROJECT - HOST LOCATION
Galilee Baptist Church
Dr. Michael T. Scott, Sr., Pastor
1216 N. Westnedge Avenue
Kalamazoo, Michigan

QUESTIONS, PLEASE CONTACT
Pamela Robinson, Doctoral Candidate
Probinson15@apexsot.edu
269-205-3356

Appendices

Appendix H

Psychotropic Medication Review Meeting

- A medication review is a doctor's appointment where you will talk to your doctor about the medication, you take each day.

- Medication reviews are important because they help the doctor know if the client's medications are helping you or not.

- Medication reviews meeting typically happens every three months. However, if the client's medication is not working, the appointment might happen sooner.

How to Prepare for a Doctor's Appointment

- Make a List and Prioritize Your Concerns
- Take Information with You to the Doctor
- Consider Bringing a Family Member or Friend to the Doctor's Visit
- Keep Your Doctor Up to Date
- Be Sure You Can See and Hear as Well As Possible
- Request an Interpreter if You Need One

Make a List and Prioritize Your Concerns

Make a list of what you want to discuss. For example, do you have a new symptom you want to ask the doctor about? Are concerned about how a treatment is affecting your daily life? If you have more than a few items to discuss, put them in order, and ask about the most important ones first. Do not put off the things that are really on your mind until the end of your appointment—bring them up right away!

Consider Bringing a Family Member or Friend to the Doctor's Office

Sometimes it is helpful to bring a family member or close friend with you. Let the family member or friend know in advance what you want from your visit. The companion can remind you what you planned to discuss with the doctor if you forget. She or he can take notes for you and can help you remember what the doctor said.

Do not let the companion take too strong a role. The visit is between you and the doctor. You may want some time alone with the doctor to discuss personal matters.

If you are alone with the doctor during or right after the physical exam, this might be a good time to raise privacy concerns. Or you could ask your family member or friend to stay in the waiting room for part of the appointment. For the best results, you should let the companion know in advance how he or she can be most helpful.

Appendices

Appendix I

Discussing Your Concerns with the Doctor Worksheet

At each visit, your doctor will likely ask about your concerns. It is a good idea to think about what you'd like to talk about before the actual visit. This form can help you organize your thoughts. Make a copy of the blank form so you will always have a clean copy to use. Then, after you make an appointment, take a minute to write down the name of the doctor and the appointment details (for example, the date, time, and address). Use the form to make a list (in order, from most important to least important) of the concerns you want to discuss.

Doctor:	Time:	Address:	Appt. Date:	Phone:

Appointment Details (Most Important to Least Important)

1	
2	
3	
4	
5	
6	
7	
8	

Notes:

Appendix J

Psychotropic Medication Review: Questions About My Mood

At my medication review meetings, the doctor might ask me about my mood, or how I feel different emotions, during the month.

She might ask: "Does your mood stay the same (stay **stable**) during the month? How does mood stabilization medication work to improve the way I feel?"

I can say: "My mood changes during the month. For 2 or 3 days in the first week or last week of the month, my mood changes. I might feel more irritable at this time. Irritable means feeling mad about things that don't bother me most of the time. I also might sleep a lot on these days. I may also be quieter and more withdrawn, and not want to talk to other people."

These changes in my mood are called **mood swings**.

My doctor might say "What things do you do to work through your feelings in a safe way and keep your mood steady?"

I can say: "I can follow my schedule, listen to gospel music, write in my journal, or take a walk. I can pray and talk to Jesus, tell my family how I feel, and finish chores. I can also read social stories, work in my A.B.A. therapy and Music Therapy meetings, and relax to help me work through my feelings. I also can exercise by swimming in the pool or riding my bike also helps stay positive and keep my mood steady.

What does Mood Stabilizing Medication do?

What are some of the side effects of mood stabilizing medication?

Appendices

Appendix K

Psychotropic Medication Review: Questions About Sleep

At my medication review meeting, my doctor might ask me about my sleep schedule.

She might ask: "How many hours do you sleep each night?"

I can answer: "I sleep for up to 8 hours each night."

She might ask: "What is your night time schedule?"

I can answer: "I eat dinner at 6 p.m., then, listen to music or do another activity. Then I take a shower, watch TV, then I got to bed at 9 p.m."

She might also ask: "What is your morning routine?"

I can say: "I wake up at about 7:30 a.m. We make breakfast together, then she or my mother helps me in the shower."

My doctor might ask: "Do you ever take naps during the day?"

I can answer: "Sometimes I take a 2 hour nap during the day. I also relax in my recliner during the day."

My doctor might ask: "Does your sleep schedule ever change during the month?"

I can answer: "Yes. My mood sometimes changes during the first week of the month, or the last week of the month, and changes how I sleep.

Sometimes I sleep too much, and sometimes I do not get much sleep.

During these times, I may wake up, eat breakfast, and then go to sleep for the rest of the day. Then I might wake up, eat dinner and shower, then go back to bed without talking to my family very much."

Appendix L

Psychotropic Medication Review: Questions about Appetite

At my medication review meeting, my doctor might ask me about my appetite.

My appetite is how much or how little I want to eat during the day.

My doctor might ask, "How has your appetite been since we last talked?"

I can answer, "My appetite has been good during most of the month. On most days, I love to eat and have large portions.

Sometimes my appetite is poor and I don't feel very hungry, sometimes my family has to encourage me to eat.

Will the Anti depressant that I am taking cause weight gain?

Does the medication I'm taking cause increased energy and reduced appetite?

How can I control my appetite while on antidepressants?

How can I fighting medication-induced weight gain?

Appendices

Appendix M

Psychotropic Medication Review: Questions on Focus & Direction Following

At my medication review meeting, my doctor might ask me questions about my focus and following directions.

At my meeting, my doctor might ask, "Are you able to focus and finish tasks at home?"

I can say, "Yes! I can focus and finish things without incident."

My doctor might also ask, "Have there been any big changes in your life? How do you feel about them?"

I can say "Yes. I have started online counseling one day per week. I feel comfortable and okay with the changes in my schedule because of the Coronavirus."

My doctor might also ask, "What things help you feel better when things in your life change?"

I can say, "Following my schedule, listening to music, resting, and journaling help me feel better. Taking walks, praying, and talking to my family also help me. Working with my music therapist and A.B.A. therapist help me too.

Are you feeling forgetful and having trouble focusing?

Do you find it difficult to concentrate on work assignments or to carry out other everyday activities?

Do you worry excessively, expect the worst, or are constantly on edge?

Definitions

African American - An American of African and especially of Black African descent.

African American (Black) church - A group of individuals attending a Christian based church of a historically African American denomination and/or predominately African American congregation.

Anxiety Disorder - A state of intense, often disabling apprehension, uncertainty, and fear caused by the anticipation of something threatening.

Bipolar Disorder - Mania is the term psychiatrists use to describe a state of elevated mood, rapid speech, grandiose thinking, and agitation that can occur in several different, but which is the hallmark of bipolar disorder, previously known as manic-depressive illness.

Black - Relating to any of various population groups having dark pigmentation of the skin.

Clergy - Designated or appointed leaders of a faith-based organization or religious group who help individuals come together under one faith as a group. For the purposes of this project, clergy was considered synonymous with the terms pastor, minister, bishop, or preacher.

Clinical social worker - A social worker trained in psychotherapy who helps individuals deal with a variety of mental health and daily living problems to improve overall functioning. A social worker usually has a master's degree in social work and has studied sociology, growth and development, mental health theory and practice.

Congregants - A person who is part of a congregation: a person who is attending religious services or who regularly attends religious services.

Dementia - The deterioration of intellectual faculties resulting from a disorder of the brain and often accompanied by emotional disturbance.

Depression - A mental health disorder characterized by persistently depressed mood or loss of interest in activities, causing significant impairment in daily life.

Definitions

Developmental Disability - Having a physical or mental impairment (such as mental retardation, autism, cerebral palsy, or spina bifida) that becomes apparent shortly after birth or during childhood and delays, prevents, or limits progression of normal development (as in language, learning, or mobility).

Diagnosis - The art or act of identifying a disease from its signs and symptoms. Graves disease. A swelling of the neck and protrusion of the eyes resulting from an overactive thyroid gland.

Hyperthyroidism - Overactivity of the thyroid gland, resulting in a rapid heartbeat and an increased rate of metabolism.

Intellectual Disability - Having slow mental development.

Manic Depression - An affective disorder marked by alternating episodes of mania and depression.

Misdiagnosis - An incorrect diagnosis of an illness or other problem.

Mood Disorder - A mental illness in which people experience severe disturbances in their feelings and general state of mind.

Psychiatrists - A physician who specializes in the prevention, diagnosis, and treatment of mental illness. A psychiatrist must receive additional training and serve a supervised residency in his or her specialty. He or she may also have additional training in a psychiatric specialty, such as child psychiatry or neuropsychiatry. Psychiatrists can prescribe medication, which psychologists cannot do.

Mania - A mental disorder that involves extreme optimism and excessive energy, often accompanied by uncontrollable irritability and anger.

Mental Illness - A mental, behavioral, or emotional disorder resulting in serious functional impairment, which substantially interferes with or limits one or more major life activities.

Religion - A personal set or institutionalized system of religious attitudes, beliefs, and practices.

Schizophrenia - Schizophrenia presents as a chronic, often debilitating mental disorder distinguished by cognitive, affective, and behavioral alterations.

Spiritual - Relating to, consisting of, or affecting the spirit or, alternatively, concerned with religious values.

Spiritual assessment - The process by which health care providers can identify a patient's spiritual needs pertaining to their mental health care.

Spirituality - A broad concept with room for many perspectives. In general, it includes a sense of connection to something bigger than ourselves, and it typically involves a search for meaning in life.

Reference List

2018 National Healthcare Quality and Disparities Report. Content last reviewed April 2020. Agency for Healthcare Research and Quality, Rockville, MD. https://www.ahrq.gov/research/findings/nhqrdr/nhqdr18/index.html.

Akutsu, P. D., Snowden, L. R., & Organista, K. C. Referral patterns to ethnic-specific and mainstream mental health programs for Hispanics and non-Hispanic Whites. 43 Journal of Counseling Psychology, . (1996):56–64.

Altshuler, S. Child well-being in kinship foster care: Similar to, or different from, non-related foster care? 20 Children and Youth Services Review, (1998):369–388.

American Psychological Association. (2017). Demographic characteristics of APA members by membership characteristics. Retrieved from https://www.apa.org/workforce/publications/17-member-profiles/table-1.pdf.

American Psychiatric Association. (2017). Mental Health Disparities: African Americans. Retrieved from https://www.psychiatry.org/File percent20Library/Psychiatrists/Cultural-Competency/Mental-Health-Disparities/Mental-Health-Facts-for-African-Americans.pdf.

American Psychiatric Association. (2013). Diagnostic and statistical manual of mental disorders (5th ed.). Washington, DC: Publisher.

Asher R. Myxoedematous madness. Br Med J. 1949;2:555–562. [PMC free article] [PubMed] [Google Scholar].

Baillargeon, J., Penn, J. V., Thomas, C. R., Temple, J. R., Baillargeon, G., & Murray, O. J. (2009). Psychiatric disorders and suicide in the nation's largest state prison system. The journal of the American Academy of Psychiatry and the Law, 37(2), 188–193.

Baker, F. M. Black youth suicide: Literature review with a focus on prevention. 82 Journal of the National Medical Association, . (1990):495–507. [PMC free article] [PubMed].

Baker, F. M., & Bell, C. C. Issues in the psychiatric treatment of African Americans. 50, Psychiatric Services, (1999):362–368. [PubMed].

Baker, F. M., Stokes-Thompson, J., Davis, O. A., Gonzo, R., & Hishinuma, E. S. Two-year outcomes of psychosocial rehabilitation of black clients with chronic mental illness. 50, Psychiatric Services, (1999):535–539. [PubMed].

Barrett, D. F., Anolik, I., & Abramson, F. H (1992, August) The 1990 Census shelter and street night enumeration Paper presented at the American Statistical Association Annual Meetings, Boston, MA.

Becerra, R. M., & Inlehart, A. P. Folk medicine use: Diverse populations in a metropolitan area. 21 Social Work in Health Care, (1995):37–52.[PubMed].

Bell, C.C. Stress-related disorders in African American children. 89, Journal of the National Medical Association, (1997):335–340 [PMC free article] [PubMed].

Bell, C.C., Dixie-Bell, D. D., & Thompson, B. Further studies on the prevalence of isolated sleep paralysis in black subjects. 78 Journal of the National Medical Association, (1986):649–659 [PMC free article] [PubMed].

Bell, C.C., & Fink, P. J. (2000)In C. Bell (Ed.), Psychiatric aspects of violence:
Issues in prevention and treatment (New Directions for Mental Health Services, 86), San Francisco Jossey Bass.

Bell, C.C., Shakoor, B., Thompson, B., Dew, D., Hughley, E., Mays, R., & Shorter-Gooden, K. Prevalence of isolated sleep paralysis in black subjects. 76 Journal of the National Medical Association, (1984):501–508. [PMC free article] [PubMed]

Berrick, J., Barth, R., & Needell, B. A. Comparison of kinship foster homes and foster family homes: Implications for kinship foster care as family preservation. 16 Children and Youth Services Review, (1994):33–64.

Black, B. S., Rabins, P. V., German, P., McGuire, M., & Roca, R. Need and unmet need for mental health care among elderly public housing residents. 37 The Gerontologist, . (1997):717–728 [PubMed].

Blazer, D. G., Hybels, C. F., Simonsick, E. M., & Hanlon, J. T. Marked differences in antidepressant use by race in an elderly community sample: 1986-1996. 157 American Journal of Psychiatry, . (2000):1089–1094. [PubMed]

Blazer, D. G., Landerman, L. R., Hays, J. C., Simonsick, E. M., & Saunders, W. B. Symptoms of depression among community-dwelling elderly African-American adults. 28 Psychological Medicine, . (1998):1311–1320. [PubMed].

Bureau of Justice Statistics. (2018). Prisoners in 2016. Retrieved from https://www.bjs.gov/content/pub/pdf/p16.pdf.

Burke J. The effect of patient race and socio-economic status on physicians' perceptions of patients. Soc Sci Med. 2000;50(6):813–828.

Burgess DJ, Fu SS, van Ryn MJ Gen Intern Med. 2004 Nov; 19(11):1154-9.

Chris Oneth Lmft Counseling & Consulting, http://chrisoneth.com/blog/the-hand-off-when-pastors-should-refer, 2020

Elbogen, E. B., & Johnson, S. C. (2009, February 10). Mental illness by itself does not predict future violent behavior. Retrieved from http://news.unchealthcare.org/som-vital-signs/2009/february/unc-study-mental-illness-by-itself-does-not-predict-future-violent-behavior.

Reference List

Eliminating Barriers to the Treatment of Mental Illness. 13 Sept. 2016, www.easybib.com/mla8-format/online-database-citation.

Hor, K., & Taylor, M. (2010). Suicide and schizophrenia: a systematic review of rates and risk factors. Journal of psychopharmacology (Oxford, England), 24(4 Suppl), 81–90. https://doi.org/10.1177/1359786810385490 https://youtu.be/F3wwUdanYY4. (1996, August 21). Prodigal Son [Video].

Hammond, Fred, Radical for Christ. https://youtu.be/F3wwUdanYY4.

Grier, H. C. P. W. H. M. (1968). *Black Rage, Two Black Psychiatrists Tell it as it is* (Fifth Impression ed.). NY Basic Books C.

Gull WW. On cretinoid state supervening in adult life in women. Trans Clinical Society of London. 1874;7:180–185. [Google Scholar] http://www.census.gov/newsroom/releases/archives/2010_census/cb11-cn185.html.

Johnson, John. "Jail Suicides Reach Record Pace in State." *Los Angeles Times*, June 16, 2002.

Kaiser Family Foundation. (2020). *Changes in Health Coverage by Race and Ethnicity since the ACA, 2010-2018*. Retrieved from https://www.kff.org/disparities-policy/issue-brief/changes-in-health-coverage-by-race-and-ethnicity-since-the-aca-2010-2018/.

Lambert, Tom. An Inclusive Church Is Like a Stained Glass Window, Archdiocese of Chicago, Commission on Mental Illness, 2017.

Lambert, Tom. Mental Illness and Faith Community Support For Recovery, Archdiocese of Chicago, Commission on Mental Illness, 2015.

Larimore WL. (2001).Providing basic spiritual care for patients: should it be the exclusive domain of pastoral professionals? American Family Physician, 63(1):36-40.

Le Cook B., Manning W., Alegria M. Measuring disparities across the distribution of mental health care expenditures. The Journal of Mental Health Policy and Economics. 2013 Mar;16(1):3-12.

Lukachko A, Myer I, Hankerson S. Religiosity and Mental Health Service Utilization Among African-Americans. J Nerv Ment Dis. 2015;203(8):578-582. doi:10.1097/NMD.0000000000000334.

Mayo RM, Sherrill WW, Sundareswaran P, Crew L. Attitudes and perceptions of Hispanic patients and health care providers in the treatment of Hispanic patients: a review of the literature. Hisp Health Care Int. 2007;5(2):64–72.

McGaffee, J., Barnes, M. A., & Lippmann, S. (1981). Psychiatric presentations of hypothyroidism. American family physician, 23(5), 129–133.

Mental Health By the Numbers [Web log post]. (2019, September 15). Retrieved from https://www.nami.org/mhstats.

Murray, G. R. (1891). Note on the Treatment of Myxoedema by Hypodermic Injections of an Extract of the Thyroid Gland of a Sheep. BMJ, 2(1606), 796–797.Ord WM. On myxoedema. R Med Chir Soc Trans. 1878;61:57–78.

National Guidelines for Behavioral Health Crisis Care Best Practice Toolkit (National Guidelines for Crisis Care), Substance Abuse and Mental Health Services Administration (SAMHSA), U.S. Department of Health and Human Services, Rockville, MD, 2020.

Prison Policy Initiative. United States Profile: Racial and Ethnic Disparities in Prisons and Jails. Retrieved from https://www.prisonpolicy.org/profiles/US.html#disparities.

Psychol Serv. 2014 Nov;11(4):357-68. doi: 10.1037/a0038122. Toward culturally centered integrative care for addressing mental health disparities among ethnic minorities.

Ranganath KA, Nosek BA. Implicit attitudes. In: Baumeister RF, Vohs KD, editors. Encyclopedia of Social Psychology. Thousand Oaks, CA: Sage Publications; 2007. pp. 465–467.

Report of the Committee of the Clinical Society of London to investigate the subject of myxoedema. Trans Clinical Society of London. 1888 21(suppl). 1–215. [Google Scholar].

SAMHSA. 2018 National Survey on Drug Use and Health (NSDUH): African Americans. https://www.samhsa.gov/data/sites/default/files/reports/rpt23247/2_AfricanAmerican_2020_01_14_508.pdf.

Serious Mental Illness Prevalence in Jails and Prisons. 13 Sept. 2016, www.treatmentadvocacycenter.org/evidence-and-research/learn-more-about/3695.

Shrivastava A, Jadhav V, Karia S, Shah N, De Sousa A. Serum thyroid stimulating hormone levels and suicidal tendency in patients with first-episode schizophrenia: An exploratory study. Thyroid Res Pract 2016;13:63-6. Back to cited text no. 1.

Smedley BD, Stith AY, Nelson AR. Unequal Treatment: Confronting Racial and Ethnic Disparities in Health Care. Washington, DC: National Academies Press; 2003.

Smedley B, Stith AY, Nelson AR. Unequal Treatment: Confronting Racial and Ethnic Disparities in Health Care. Institute of Medicine of the National Academie; 2002.

Snyder, A. (2020). *Black Mental Health Matters: The Ultimate Guide for Mental Health Awareness in the Black Community.* Toledo, OH: Majestic

Swink, D. F. (2010, October 19). Communicating with People With Mental Illness: The Public's Guide. Retrieved from https://www.psychologytoday.com/us/blog/threat-management/201010/communicating-people-mental-illness-the-publics-guide.

Tachman ML, Guthrie GP Jr. Hypothyroidism: diversity of presentation. Endocr Rev. 1984;5:456–465. [PubMed] [Google Scholar].

Unconscious (implicit) bias and health disparities: where do we go from here? Blair IV, Steiner JF, Havranek EP Perm J. 2011 Spring; 15(2):71-8.

Reference List

United States Census Bureau. (2019). Income and Poverty in the United States: 2018. Retrieved from https://www.census.gov/content/dam/Census/library/publications/2019/demo/p60-266.pdf.

United States Census Bureau. (2019). Quick facts. Retrieved fromhttps://www.census.gov/quickfacts/fact/table/US/PST120219.

Wang, P. S., Berglund, P. A., & Kessler, R. C. (2003). Patterns and correlates of contacting clergy for mental disorders in the United States. Health services research, 38(2), 647–673. https://doi.org/10.1111/1475-6773.00138.

Ward, E. C., Wiltshire, J. C., Detry, M. A., & Brown, R. L. (2013). African American men and women's attitude toward mental illness, perceptions of stigma, and preferred coping behaviors. Nursing Research >, 62 >(3), 185-194. doi:10.1097/NNR.0b013e31827bf533.

Weaver AJ, Koenig HG. Religion, spirituality, and their relevance to medicine: an update. Am Fam Physician. 2006;73(8):1336-1337.

Westphal SA. Unusual presentations of hypothyroidism. Am J Med Sci. 1997;314:333–337. [PubMed] [Google Scholar].

Williams, M. T. (2011). Why African Americans avoid psychotherapy. Psychology Today. Retrieved from https://www.psychologytoday.com/us/blog/culturally-speaking/201111/why-african-americans-avoid-psychotherapy.

Yzerbyt VY, Rogier A, Fiske ST. Group entitativity and social attribution: on translating situational constraints into stereotypes. Pers Soc Psychol Bull. 1998;24(10):1089–1103.

Recommended Reading

Alexander, Michelle, *The New Jim Crow*, The New Press, New York, 2012.
American community. Deviant Behavior, American Psychological Association, 2020.
Anderson, Tonya D., *Blossoming Hope The Black Christian Woman's Guide to Mental Health and Wellness*, Overflowing Media, North Carolina, 2018.
Baldwin, Jennifer, *Trauma-Sensitive Theology: Thinking Theologically in the Era of Trauma*, Georgia, Wipf and Stock Publishers, 2018.
Boyd-Franklin, Nancy, Franklin, A.J., Toussaint, Pamela, *Boys into Men: Raising Our African American Teenaged Sons*, Dutton, New York, 2000.
Cone, James H., *God of the Oppressed*, Orbis Books, New York, 1999.
Fernando, Suman, *Institutional Racism in Psychiatry and Clinical Psychology*, Springer International Publishing, Switzerland, 2017.
Frances, Allen, *Essentials of Psychiatric Diagnosis: Responding to the Challenge of DSM-5*, New York, Guilford Press, 2013.
Franklin-Boyd, Nancy, *Black Families in Therapy*, New York, Guilford Press, 2003.
Franklin-Boyd, Nancy, *Black Families in Therapy: A Multisystems Approach*, New York, Guilford Press, 1989.
Griffith M.D, Ezra E. H., Jones M.D., Billy E., Stewart M.D., Altha J., Black Mental Health, Patients, Providers, and Systems, Psychiatric Association Publishing, 2019.
Head, John, *Black Men and Depression*, Harlem Moon, New York, 2004.
Iwamasa, Gayle Y., Hays, Pamela A., *Culturally Responsive Cognitive Behavioral Therapy*, American Psychological Association, Washington, 2019.
Jackson, L. C., & Greene, *Psychotherapy with African American Women: Innovations in Psychodynamic Perspectives and Practice*, Guilford Press, New York, 2000.
Jackson, L. C., & Greene, Beverly, *Psychodynamic Perspectives and Practice*, Gilford Press, New York, 2000.
Jones, Charisse, Gooden-Shorter, Kumea, *Shifting*, Harper Collins Publishers, New York, 2003.
Leigh, Angelica, *Black Girls Don't Cry*, Angelica Leigh Wilson, Illinois, 2012.
Nouwen, Heni J.M., *The Wounded Healer*, Image Books, New York, 1979.
Suskind, Ron, *A Hope in the Unseen*, Broadway Books, New York, 1999.
Synyder, Aaren, *Black Mental Health Matters*, Majestic Publishing, Ohio, 2020.
Ward, Janie Victoria, *The Skin We're In: Teaching Our Children to be Emotionally Strong, Socially Smart, Spiritually Connected*, The Free Press, New York, 2000.
Walker, Rheeda, *The Unapologetic Guide to Black Mental Health*, New Harbinger Publications, Inc., California, 2020.
Williams, Terrie M., *Black Pain: It Just Looks Like We're Not Hurting*, New York, Simon and Schuster, 2009.

About the Author

As a Christian, Dr. Pamela Robinson has come to know the Lord Jesus Christ as a comforter and a guide; one who will never leave nor forsake her. She believes that it is a humbling experience to work with individuals during their times of difficulty. Knowing that the emotions and behaviors of those suffering can be intense, she understands that during times of crisis, many people just want the pain to end and have the problem resolved. In addition, she feels a special calling to help during those difficult times and feels honored when invited to help them make changes in their lives.

As a Clinical Social Worker and Pastoral Theologian, Dr. Robinson is the Founder of Emerging HOPE Christian Counseling in Kalamazoo, Michigan an interdisciplinary private practice which provides culturally relevant mental health services and programming in partnership with clients. She is the co-founder and co-pastor of Emerging HOPE Ministries in Kalamazoo, Michigan a family-fortifying ministry whose mission is to make disciples by declaring the gospel of Jesus Christ in the power of the Spirit and gather those disciples into the church, that they might worship the Lord and obey his commands now and in eternity to the glory of God the Father.

As a marketplace entrepreneur and pastoral theologian, she focuses on media educational outreach, collaboration with marketplace business establishments, and educational empowerment by preaching the gospel, evangelizing, conducting educational workshops, and seminars across the country.

Dr. Robinson is a field instructor for Western Michigan University's School of Social Work in Kalamazoo, Michigan. Her counseling practice provides undergraduate and masters-level social work students with valuable experiences to complete their degree. The esteemed author has self published a parenting educational curriculum, *Emerging HOPE Parenting Manual*, and the cutting-edge dissertation, "Educating the African American Church Toward Those with Mental Health Challenges to Have an Attitudinal Change."

The focal point of the Emerging HOPE ministry logo is the Lotus flower. Of all the plants in the world, the lotus flower is the most unique. It grows in

About the Author

muddy waters and rises through the murky waters to bloom into a beautiful pink and white flower. It signifies strength as it moves from the dark into the light. It also symbolizes inner strength in that it shows the determination to come out of difficulties.

Dr. Robinson's life exemplifies this beautiful resilient flower. She is not afraid of treading the road less traveled and prides herself on being able to thrive in adverse conditions. Just like the Lotus flower, Dr. Robinson's life is a blend of beauty, determination, and courage.

She is happily married to Reverend Curtis L. Robinson, Sr. They have a blended family of six adult children, many grandchildren, and one incredibly special grandson, Zecaryah. The Robinsons resides in Kalamazoo, Michigan.

Book Reviews

You will find Dr. Pamela Robinson's book very practical as she writes with passion and understanding from both lived and professional experience. Her desire to educate and affect community acceptance of people with disabilities is a result of diverse field research and community outreach. She challenges all people and desires to equip the church, faith and professional communities to offer unconditional love through breaking ethnic, socioeconomic and racial barriers. There is no greater need today than to share God's wholeness and love with broken people!

Sara L. Collison
Co-author of *What Is In Your Hand? A Journey Toward Shalom,* and *Co-founder of SHALOM INC. of Kalamazoo, Michigan, a nonprofit organization that serves adults with disabilities.*

Nobody wants to admit to themselves that they are vulnerable and hurting inside, let alone confess to someone else. Walking around pretending that nothing is wrong will not make the pain go away. I have firsthand experience in dealing with mental health in the church as my young adult daughter dealt with depression and was suicidal for many years. This is while she was faithfully singing and leading others into the presence of God with worship. It was only through the grace of God and a good spiritual based counselor that she is now delivered and successfully pursuing God's plan for her life. But because of the stress of dealing with my daughter and the challenges of my life, I found it necessary to seek out counseling.

The Color of HOPE provides needed answers to family members who often are challenged with mental health issues and find themselves in need of support. This book speaks directly to our issues and compels us to unlock the door of the mysterious "taboo" topic—mental illness and the Black church.

Dr. Pamela Robinson is a pioneer in addressing the stigma regarding mental health in the Black church. *The Color of HOPE* is a catalyze to blaze the trail of eradicating mental health stigma.

Dorla E. Coleman-Bonner, MTS, Licensed Elder
Director of Diversity Equity and Inclusion for The City of Kalamazoo, Michigan; Apex School of Theology Doctoral Committee member for Dr. Pamela Robinson

I applaud Dr. Pamela Robinson for standing up and addressing the issue of mental health wellness in the Black community. *The Color of HOPE* brings a new understanding to the widely held misconceptions and stigma about mental illness. It is very encouraging to see how *The Color of HOPE* was strategically written to impact the lives of so many, especially individuals and families in need of mental health services.

Whether it is related to guidance, personal resources, mental health services, connection to community resources or advocacy *The Color of HOPE* succinctly addresses these issues. *The Color of HOPE* is a compilation of the work that Dr. Pamela Robinson has worked effortless in the trenches over the last twenty years to birth. This cutting-edge book compels us to remove our masks, freeing us to dive into often unchartered territory as we boldly face the issue of mental health wellness.

Lesa Ann Henry, LLMSW
Licensed Minister, Mental Health Advocate, Clinical Social Worker

Dr. Robinson deftly takes us on a cultural journey into the controlled environment of the prison where too many of our African American Men are reentering back into society without getting their mental health needs met. These men are subjected to recidivism, homelessness, police brutality, etc. because they do not get the help they need inside the penal system or outside once released back into society.

The Color of HOPE sheds light on this reprehensible issue and needs of our African American men as far as mental health is concerned. This is a must-read for black men suffering with "closeted" mental health issues.

Gregory E. Haymon
Clinical Social Worker, MSW, LCSW

If an ounce of demonstration is worth a ton of speculation, the story which Dr. Pamela Robinson tells is precious, indeed. Dr. Robinson has used her personal, spiritual, and professional journey in experiencing the challenges and joys of dealing with individuals with mental health challenges.

She has literally taken Jesus' mandate to us in Luke 4:18-19, KJV 18 The Spirit of the Lord is upon me, because he hath anointed me to preach the gospel to the poor; he hath sent me to heal the brokenhearted, to preach deliverance to the captives, and recovering of sight to the blind, to set at liberty them that are bruised, 19 To preach the acceptable year of the Lord. Her book has "opened eyes that we may see, and made the Biblical Scripture come alive to the reader."

It is encouraging to know that the book, "The Color of HOPE" African American Mental Health in the Church, is not a denominational book, but universal for all Christendom to teach to their ministers and laity how to receive an understanding of our mission and to have an attitudinal change towards individuals who are challenged with mental disabilities.

I appreciate the thoroughness of her extensive research to equip the pastors with the necessary tools to transform churches into a spiritual institute of hospitality and love to welcome children and adults into God's Houses of worship.

With a mindset of love and understanding, we can truly become a change agent for change, heal the brokenhearted, to preach deliverance to the captives, and recovering of sight to the blind, to set at liberty them that are bruised, 19 To preach the acceptable year of the Lord. This book should be on the bookshelves of clergy, all colleges, and universities of theology.

Pastor Bobette Hampton
Fresh Fire AME Church, Kalamazoo, Michigan

www.ingramcontent.com/pod-product-compliance
Lightning Source LLC
Chambersburg PA
CBHW060835050426
42453CB00008B/703